which Prince and her
siblings were put up ... ... sold to the brutal Captain
I—, and then to Mr D—, who took her to the Turks Islands to work
in the salt ponds. In 1815 she was sold to John Wood and taken to
Antigua. At about this time Prince joined the Moravian church, where
she met Daniel James, a freeman, whom she married in 1826.

In 1828 Prince was taken to England by Mr and Mrs Wood. In
November of that year, she reported to the Anti-Slavery Society in
Aldermanbury, east London, that she had been ill-treated by the
Woods, and she exercised her right to freedom under English law.
However, this right was only valid while she remained in England, and
Prince had to choose whether to remain a freewoman in England or
return to her husband in Antiqua as a slave. She decided to stay, and
in 1829 she was employed as a domestic servant by Thomas Pringle,
the secretary of the Anti-Slavery Society. Prince dictated her *History*
to Susannah Strickland, an acquaintance of the Pringles, and it was
published in 1881, running to three editions that year. An article,
published in *Blackwood's Magazine* and casting doubt on the authenticity of Prince's story, led Pringle to successfully sue the publisher of
the magazine in 1833, and later that year Wood brought a libel case
against Pringle. Prince gave evidence at both trials.

It is thought that Prince remained in England after 1833, perhaps
continuing to work as a servant. Her *History* is an important contribution to early black writing, and it offers a glimpse into the lives of
enslaved men and women whose life stories cannot be traced.

SARA SALIH is currently a lecturer in English at Wadham College,
Oxford. Her PhD thesis was on gender performance in Frances
Burney's novels, and she has published on 'race' and the eighteenth-
century novel. She is currently writing a book on Judith Baker.

THE HISTORY OF
MARY PRINCE

A WEST INDIAN SLAVE

Edited by SARA SALIH

PENGUIN BOOKS

PENGUIN BOOKS

Published by the Penguin Group
Penguin Books Ltd, 27 Wrights Lane, London W8 5TZ, England
Penguin Putnam Inc., 375 Hudson Street, New York, New York 10014, USA
Penguin Books Australia Ltd, Ringwood, Victoria, Australia
Penguin Books Canada Ltd, 10 Alcorn Avenue, Toronto, Ontario, Canada M4V 3B2
Penguin Books (NZ) Ltd, Private Bag 102902, NSMC, Auckland, New Zealand

Penguin Books Ltd, Registered Offices: Harmondsworth, Middlesex, England

First published in 1831
Published in Penguin Books 2000
1 3 5 7 9 10 8 6 4 2

Editorial matter copyright © Sara Salih, 2000
All rights reserved

The moral right of the editor has been asserted

Set in 10/12.5 pt Adobe Caslon
Typeset by Rowland Phototypesetting Ltd, Bury St Edmunds, Suffolk
Printed in England by Clays Ltd, St Ives plc

CONTENTS

ACKNOWLEDGEMENTS

I am very grateful to the librarians at Rhodes House and the Bodleian Library, Oxford, where most of the research for this edition was carried out, as well as the British Library and the Archive at Birmingham Public Library. I am also grateful to Jeff Howarth, Information Officer at the Anti-Slavery Society, for fetching and carrying books for me, and to Caroline Moorhead who supplied me with information about the foundation of the Anti-Slavery Society. Stephen Ellison, in the Record Office at the House of Lords, provided me with a copy of the report of the petition that was presented to Parliament on Mary Prince's behalf in 1829, and Vernon Nelson at the Moravian Archive in Bethlehem, Pennsylvania, hunted for a record of Prince's marriage in the 'Spring Gardens Banns'.

Moira Ferguson's edition of the *History* has been very useful, as have Vincent Carretta's exemplary editions of Olaudah Equiano's *Interesting Narrative* and Ignatius Sancho's *Letters*. Robert Mighall at Penguin has been an excellent editor, and thanks are due to Judith Hawley, Adam Roberts and Shaen Catherwood who helped me to track down references, or pointed me in the right direction – as did Warwick Thompson (as ever).

INTRODUCTION

'De nigger woman is de mule uh de world so fur as Ah can see.'
Zora Neale Hurston, *Their Eyes Were Watching God* (1937)

MARY PRINCE'S LIFE

Mary Prince's *History* is the first narrative of the life of a black woman to be published in England. In 1828 Mary Prince made her way to the offices of the Anti-Slavery Society in Aldermanbury, east London, where she reported that she had been ill-treated by her current master and mistress who had brought her to England with them on a trip from Antigua. Prince had worked for Mr and Mrs Wood for about thirteen years, and she had been eager to accompany them on their trip to London because she believed she might find a cure for her rheumatism there. However, on arriving she suffered an acute attack which made it painful for her to wash the large piles of clothes they gave her, but the Woods ignored her complaints and continued to work her as hard as ever, repeatedly threatening to turn her out of doors if she did not do as she was told. This finally proved too much for Prince, and she left the Woods and went to lodge with a Mr Mash, the shoe-cleaner, and his wife. Eventually she appealed to Christian missionaries for help, and when a woman called Hill told her about the Anti-Slavery Society, she travelled to their headquarters in east London to ask for legal advice.

Prince reached Aldermanbury by a circuitous route, via Bermuda, the Turks and Caicos Islands (Prince talks of 'Turk's Island' – though she probably means Grand Turk – and contemporary accounts refer to them as the Turks Islands, the form that will be used here) and Antigua, so that her *History* exemplifies in miniature what Paul Gilroy has called the 'Black Atlantic', the 'intercultural and transnational formation' of culture arising, in the first instance, out of the transatlantic slave trade from the seventeenth century onwards.[1] Prince's life was indeed one of diaspora and displacement. Born in Brackish Pond, Bermuda, in 1788, she was the 'property' of a Charles Myners until she was given to Captain Williams, a man who was just as cruel as the subsequent masters she was to serve. At least Williams's wife and daughter treated Prince with kindness, and she was also relatively happy when she was temporarily hired out to Mrs Pruden, whose daughter Fanny initiated an informal course of reading. '[H]er method of teaching me was as follows,' Prince says of Fanny: 'Directly she had said her lessons to her grandmamma, she used to come running to me, and make me repeat them one by one after her, and in a few months I was able not only to say my letters but to spell many small words.' These early years were the happiest of Prince's life, since as she herself comments, she 'was too young to understand rightly [her] condition as a slave, and too thoughtless and full of spirits to look forward to the days of toil and sorrow.' However, the idyll was interrupted by Mrs Williams's death, after which Prince and her siblings were 'put on the market', a harrowing scene which she describes with characteristic vivacity and feeling:

I cannot bear to think of that day, – it is too much. – It recalls the great grief that filled my heart, and the woeful thoughts that passed to and fro through my mind . . . I wish I could find words to tell you all I then felt and suffered. The great God above alone knows the thoughts of the poor slave's heart, and the bitter pains which follow such separations as these. All that we love taken away from us – Oh, it is sad, sad! and sore to be borne!

Some time between 1800 and 1815 Prince was sold to Captain I—,[2] a man whose wife matched him in brutality, and between them the pair subjected all their slaves to routine abuse and humiliation. Eventually Prince could stand it no more and she ran away to her mother, but her father returned her to Captain I—, pleading with him to 'be a kind master to her in future'. However, the I—s did not reform their behaviour, and Prince was overjoyed when she was taken to the Turks Islands, nine hundred miles from Bermuda, five years later and sold to Mr D—. It did not take her long to realize that D— was just as ruthless as her previous master, perhaps even more so: 'I hoped, when I left Capt. I—, that I should have been better off, but I found it was but going from one butcher to another,' she writes, and she goes on to describe the cool and sinister sadism of her new master whose punishments seem to have been of a sexual nature. This aspect of her treatment is diplomatically glossed over in the *History*, since Prince and her allies at the Anti-Slavery Society were probably anxious to spare the prudish sensibilities of potential readers who may have been too squeamish to face the truth about the sexual exploitation of black women by their white masters.

Mr D— put Prince to work raking in the salt ponds on the Turks Islands, a physically arduous occupation from which Prince was given no respite, even though her feet and legs were full of painful salt boils. 'Ah, poor me!' she exclaims, 'my tasks were never ended. Sick or well, it was work – work – work!' After about ten years of this hard labour, Prince returned to Bermuda with Mr D— where she was employed as a household slave. Her master's brutal behaviour did not improve, and Prince reports that on one occasion she defended his daughter from him when he attacked her in a drunken frenzy, describing also how he would abuse Prince in a subtler way by stripping naked, ordering her to bathe him and beating her if she refused to do as she was told. When she heard that a Mr John Wood was setting out for Antigua, Prince begged to be sold to him so that she could escape from her 'indecent master' as she calls him, but once in Antigua she found that her new master and mistress were just as cruel and abusive as Mr D— had been. It was at this point that Prince seems to have turned to religion for solace, and in about 1817 she joined the Moravian church, a Protestant sect with a particularly strong missionary project. At about the same time as her religious conversion Prince met her future husband, Daniel James, a freeman, and with characteristic defiance she married him in 1826 without asking her master's permission.

Two years later, Prince set out for England with the Woods, but their continuing harsh treatment led her to exercise her legal right to freedom on English soil, and it was soon after she had left their household that she first sought help from the Anti-Slavery Society. There a solicitor, the Abolitionist George Stephen, advised her that since English law did not extend to Antigua she would forfeit her freedom if she returned to the Caribbean. Prince now faced an agonizing choice: to go back to Antigua as a slave so that she could be with her husband; or to remain in England as a freewoman. A year or so elapsed before Prince approached the Anti-Slavery Society again, and during this time she attempted to make her own living, unsuccessfully it seems. Thomas Pringle, who was secretary of the Anti-Slavery Society at the time, employed her as a domestic servant in November 1829, and in 1831 Prince dictated her narrative to Susanna Strickland, a friend of the Pringles. When her *History* was published in 1831, it ran through three editions that year and it caused something of a stir. That same year, James McQueen, the editor of the *Glasgow Courier*, felt sufficiently provoked to publish an article in *Blackwood's Magazine* in which he called into question the veracity of Prince's narrative in particular and inveighed against Abolitionists in general. Pringle successfully sued Cadell, the publisher of *Blackwood's*, in February 1833, but the tables were turned when in March of that year Wood brought a libel case against Pringle which he won. Prince gave evidence at the second trial which is reported in *The Times*, 1 March 1833 (see Appendix Three), and her testimony fills in the details which were evidently considered unsuitable for inclusion in the *History*. When she took to the witness stand, Prince described her relationship with a 'Captain A—' or Abbot, with whom she said she lived for seven years and to whom she was obviously sexually attached. Indeed, she left the Moravian Society because of her connection with Captain A—, and she relates that she subsequently lived with a freeman, Oyskman, who promised to make her free. Prince told the court that she narrated all these particulars to Susanna Strickland, who, for obvious reasons, did not write them down. It was important for the Anti-Slavery Society to present Prince as sexually pure, or, at least, the object of her master's lusts rather than the sexually active person which, by her own account, she seems to have been.

After the two libel trials Prince fades from sight: in her evidence she says that she is living at the Old Bailey and still working for the Pringles, and we may assume that she remained in England, although we do not know in what capacity or where, or whether the petition that was presented to Parliament was successful. The two surviving editions of her *History* (the first and third editions) preserve a life and a voice which would otherwise have been lost, affording a glimpse into the histories of other 'asylum seekers' of this era who, unlike Prince, did not have the opportunity to record and to publicize their experiences.

THE *HISTORY* AND THE BLACK CANON

Prince's narrative is a significant early example of the literature of the Black Atlantic, taking its place alongside texts by Albert Gronniosaw, Ignatius Sancho, John Marrant, Ottobah Cugoano (or John Stuart), Olaudah Equiano and Phillis Wheatley (see Further Reading). These authors and their texts were by no means marginal, but they received widespread publicity in the closing decades of the eighteenth century: Sancho's letters had run to five editions by 1803, while Equiano's *Interesting Narrative* went through nine editions in his lifetime, partly as a result of the energies the author channelled into publicizing both himself and his text. Prince's *History* is not autobiographical in the sense that Equiano's *Interesting Narrative* is (a point to which I will return), but it none the less belongs to what is now recognized as a canon of early black writing – a body of late eighteenth- and early nineteenth-century texts which are connected to each other as much by virtue of their subject matter and form as by their authorship.

The texts in this early black canon differ from each other in numerous obvious ways (formally, stylistically, in terms of their subject matter, for example), but there are also important parallels between, for example, Equiano's *Interesting Narrative*, Gronniosaw's *Narrative* and Cugoano's polemical *Thoughts and Sentiments*. While Equiano and Gronniosaw both use the trope of the 'talking book' to describe their first encounters with reading, Cugoano and Equiano include graphic descriptions of the iniquitous Middle Passage from the west coast of Africa to the slave plantations in the Caribbean; all three authors, along with Ignatius Sancho, express their outrage at the slave trade. In the words of Sancho to one of his English correspondents:

I say it is with reluctance, that I must observe your country's conduct has been uniformly wicked in the East – West Indies – and even on the coast of Guinea. The grand object of English navigators – indeed of all christian navigators – is money – money – money . . . In Africa, the poor wretched natives – blessed with the most fertile and luxuriant soil – are rendered so much the more miserable for what Providence meant as a blessing: – the Christians' abominable traffic for slaves – and the horrid cruelty and treachery of the petty Kings – encouraged by their Christian customers . . . But enough – it is a subject that sours my blood.[3]

The subject was certainly blood-curdling enough, and Mary Prince does not flinch from detailing what she calls 'the horrors of slavery' – the pain she suffered on being separated from her family in Bermuda, the punishments to which she was subjected by a succession of owners, the physical hardships she was forced to endure. The purpose of the text was not cathartic but documentary, and Prince's narrative is a testament to the sufferings of both herself and other slaves whose misery she witnessed.

In *Loose Canons: Notes on the Culture Wars*, Henry Louis Gates discusses the significance of early black writing and canon formation, quoting the American philosopher and poet Ralph Waldo Emerson on the subject. 'Language . . . must be raked,' writes Emerson, 'the secrets of slaughter-houses and infamous holes that cannot front the day, must be ransacked, to tell what negro slavery has been'.[4] Gronniosaw, Cugoano, Equiano and Prince are engaged in precisely such an exercise of raking and ransacking, and their texts articulate the sufferings of what would otherwise have been a forgotten generation. As Gates observes, 'black writers wrote as if their lives depended on it and, in a curious sense, their lives did, the "life" of "the race" in Western discourse'.[5] By publishing her life story, Prince engages in two kinds of 'life-saving', writing herself and her people into existence and thus preserving 'the life of the race' and writing to save her own life. The *History* is simultaneously a bid for emancipation and a protest against the slave trade, as well as representing a potential source of income for its author, whose health, as Pringle tells us, was failing.

Unlike Gronniosaw and Equiano, whose texts announce on the title page that they are 'narrated by themselves', the *History* is not a straightforward autobiography, but a collection of texts. Prince's story is mediated to us via the pen of Susanna Strickland, a friend of Thomas Pringle's, and the text itself is bolstered by an editorial supplement and appendices, an apparatus almost equal to the narrative in length that is designed to validate Prince's 'testimony'. Thomas Pringle goes out of his way to assure the reader that the body of the *History* is all Mary's own. '[The narrative] was written out fully, with all the narrator's repetitions and prolixities,' he states in his Preface, 'and afterwards pruned into its present shape; retaining, as far as was practicable, Mary's exact expressions and peculiar phraseology.' In spite of these disclaimers, it is none the less possible to detect notable shifts in register, and there are times when Prince's voice seems more discernible than at others (towards the end of her narrative, for example, where the syntax and idiom convey her palpable outrage at the mistreatment to which she has been subjected). It is also important to bear in mind that the *History* is a piece of propaganda and that it was certainly 'pruned' by Pringle and Strickland so that it could be used in the Anti-Slavery Society's campaign against the slave trade. The *History*, then, is not the simple narrative of a black woman's experiences, but it is a composite text that has been assembled by an editor who had a clear agenda in mind. The preface, supplement and appendices are an inseparable part of the text and merit equally close attention as Mary Prince's first-hand account of her life and sufferings.

LITERACY, AUTHENTICITY AND MIMICRY

Why, then, was this brief text (it is only twenty-three printed pages in the original) published with a sixteen-page editorial supplement, a validating appendix, and the history of another West African slave? The examples of other black writers, in particular Albert Gronniosaw and Phillis Wheatley, might provide us with an answer. When she attempted to publish her *Poems on Various Subjects* in the United States, Wheatley encountered such hostility that in 1773 she crossed the Atlantic and published the volume in England. This, says Henry Louis Gates, 'was the birth of the Afro-American literary tradition', but it could only take place after Wheatley had been examined by an 'August group' of 'Boston's most notable citizens' before she came to England to publish her poems.[6] As Gates points out, the modern reader is left to speculate as to what the eighteen-year-old African-American woman was asked by the panel, but from the letter of attestation printed with the first edition it is clear that the aim of the examination was to verify the authenticity of Wheatley's claim to the authorship of the poems. 'We whose Names are under-written,' runs the letter, 'do assure the World, that the POEMS specified in the following Pages, were (as we verily believe) written by PHILLIS, a young Negro Girl, who was but a few Years since, brought an uncultivated Barbarian from *Africa* . . . She has been examined by some of the best Judges, and is thought qualified to write them [i.e. the poems].'[7]

Phillis Wheatley was not the only black writer to undergo an examination to affirm the authorship of her text. Ukawsaw Gronniosaw's *A Narrative of the Most Remarkable Particulars in the Life of James Albert Ukawsaw Gronniosaw, an African Prince, As Related By Himself*, published a couple of years earlier than Wheatley's poems in around 1770, contains an account of Gronniosaw's seven-week long *viva* at the hands of Dutch clergymen. 'The Calvinist ministers in Holland desired to hear my experience from myself,' writes Gronniosaw, 'so I stood before thirty-eight ministers every Thursday, for seven weeks together, and they were all very well satisfied, and persuaded that I was what I pretended to be'.[8] Although Mary Prince did not undergo a verbal examination, the supplementary material framing her narrative is clearly an attempt to establish the authenticity of her life story and the truth of the details she supplies. This may reflect the low status of slave testimony in legal cases, where for a long time the word of a slave meant nothing when pitted against that of a white person, but in all three of the narratives I have cited it is not just textual truth and accuracy which are at stake in these affirmations of authorship and authenticity, but the very humanity of the black (writing) subject. Towards the end of the eighteenth century, debates about 'the Negro' raged in pseudo-scientific and anti-Abolitionist circles, as writers such as the white West Indian Edward Long set out to prove that 'Negroes' belonged to a separate species which was animal rather than human, while others, such as the Comte de Buffon, subscribed to the monogenist (same species) argument, but believed that the Negro was situated at the bottom of the human hierarchy.[9] 'For my own part,' writes Long in his notorious *History of Jamaica* (1774), 'I think there are extremely potent reasons for believing, that the White and the Negroe are two distinct species.' He continues this line of argument a few pages later: 'If [the Negro] is a creature *sui generis* [of his own kind] he fills up the space between mankind and the ape, as this and the monkey tribe supply the interval that is between the oran-outang and quadrupeds.'[10]

Among the 'proofs' that Long offered for his polygenetic theory (that 'Negroes' and 'Whites' were separate species) was the spurious evidence that black Africans had no arts or sciences, and that they were incapable of attaining European levels of literacy. The example Long gave to clinch his argument was that of Francis Williams, a Jamaican born around 1700 who was sent to England by the Duke of Montagu as an experiment to see whether or not 'the Negro' was capable of intellectual improvement. Long describes Williams's 'classic instruction' at a grammar school in England, after which he went on to read maths at Cambridge University. On returning to Jamaica, he got into the habit of composing odes in Latin to successive governors of the island, and Long reprinted one of these in the third volume of his *History of Jamaica*. 'With the impartiality that becomes me, I shall endeavour to do him [Williams] all possible justice,' he writes, 'and shall leave it to the reader's opinion whether what they shall discover of his genius and intellect will be sufficient to overthrow the arguments I have before alleged, to prove an inferiority of the Negroes to the race of white men'.[11] Typically, Long's 'impartiality' does not last long. 'What woeful stuff this madrigal would be / In some starv'd hackney sonneteer, or me! / But let a *Negroe* own the happy lines, / How the wit brightens! how the style refines!' he writes after quoting the whole of Williams's ode, both in Latin and in translation, and he concludes the chapter with more jaunty versifying of his own: 'The general *order*, since the whole began, / Is kept in *nature*, and is kept in *man*. *Order* is heaven's first law; and, this confest, / Some *are*, and *must be, greater* than the rest'.[12]

Long cites with approval the philosopher David Hume's retort that Williams (and, by implication, all black authors) was no more than a parrot who had merely learned to mimic the discourse of his master,[13] and this may give us some insight into the importance of the supplementary material accompanying Prince's *History*, as well as the 'examinations' Wheatley and Gronniosaw underwent in the 1770s. For clearly the 'writing Negro' contradicted contemporary beliefs in racial inferiority, dealing a serious blow to the polygenetic theories propounded by writers such as Long, who were forced to defend their beliefs by concluding that black literacy was no more than mimicry. Not only was it crucial for the editor of the *History* to prove that it was 'true' (particularly since the outcome of a libel action depended on the authenticity of Prince's allegations against her owners, the Woods), but the 'truth' of Prince's humanity was itself at stake.

It is certainly possible to argue that Prince, and most of the other black writers at this time, used 'the master's pieces' (to borrow Henry Louis Gates's phrase) to express themselves, and that this in turn might constitute a mimicry of the kind that Hume finds so risible. However, this 'mimicry' could be regarded as a radical gesture, and these texts undermine the authority of colonial discourse and the validity of its (hitherto uncontested) theories by affirming both the authorship and the authentic humanity of the black subject who was still struggling for recognition from a white establishment which persisted in regarding 'negroes' as bestial.[14] The fact that black writers published at all at this early stage is in itself a radical gesture, and the use of an elevated form such as the ode or the spiritual autobiography could be regarded as an appropriation of 'white' discourse, or, to use Homi K. Bhabha's term, a mimicking of it. Mary Prince's *History* does not quite exemplify this textual radicalism, since it was not written entirely by her, and unlike Equiano's *Interesting Narrative* or Sancho's *Letters*, it is not peppered with biblical and literary allusions which 'elevate' the text and 'prove' its writer's human intelligence. None the less, telling her life story gave Prince and her supporters the opportunity to demonstrate that, contrary to contemporary belief, 'Negroes' were not merely chattels, but humans who were seriously damaged by the brutal treatment they were forced to suffer at the hands of their white masters and mistresses.

THE BLACK COMMUNITY AND THE LAW

Mary Prince may have been the first black woman to publish her life story in England, but she was certainly not the first black woman to live there. Estimates vary as to the size of the black population in Britain at this time, some commentators placing it as high as 20,000 in the mid eighteenth century, while others give more moderate estimates. A figure generally agreed upon by twentieth-century commentators is 10,000 in around 1772.[15] It is known that there were black people in Britain from at least the sixteenth century, and the black population continued to increase during the era of the transatlantic slave trade from the seventeenth century onwards, as slave owners and white West Indians brought their 'property' with them on returning to England.

As far back as 1569, it had been legally judged 'that *England* was too pure an Air for Slaves to breathe in',[16] but from the 1760s a number of famous legal cases tested that pronouncement and brought the issue of England, slaves and freedom to the fore. From an early stage, a series of acts had been passed confirming the legal status of the slave as a 'thing', a chattel, a property, and according to James Walvin, this constituted a major change in English law where there had been no basis for treating people as chattels since the decline of feudalism.[17] Under the Yorke and Talbot judgment of 1729, slaves who were brought to England from the colonies remained property in England,[18] but here property law seems to contradict early 'civil rights' law as set out by William Blackstone in his *Commentaries on the Laws of England* where, in the first chapter, 'Of the Absolute Rights of Individuals', he asserts that English laws are designed to preserve the civil liberties 'even in the meanest subject'. '[T]his spirit of liberty is so deeply implanted in our constitution, and rooted in our very soil,' writes Blackstone, 'that a slave or a negro, the moment he lands in England, falls under the protection of the laws, and so far becomes a free man; though the master's right to his service may *possibly* still continue.' He cites a case in which a number of slaves deserted from their British master in East Florida and were subsequently discovered on board a British man-of-war that was *not* in East Florida waters. The slaves could not be compelled to return to the plantation because English law applied on the ship. As Blackstone comments:

The principle of the decision was, that slavery is not a state recognized by the law of nature generally, or the law of England locally and wherever it legally exists, it does so only by the force of some local law. Whenever, therefore, a slave comes from the place, where it is recognized, into a place under the English law, he ceases to be a slave, because the local will, by the *comitas inter communitates* [agreement between communities], enforces any local law contrary to the law of nature. An English ship, or a territory newly discovered by Englishmen, are for this purpose the same as England because the English law of freedom will apply equally in each, and be the right of everyone there.[19]

Blackstone's description of English law clearly goes against the Yorke and Talbot case, as does the Somerset case of 1772. James Somerset was a slave who escaped from his master two years after he was brought to England in 1769, but he was recaptured and imprisoned on a ship bound for Jamaica. Lord Justice Mansfield, who was presiding over the case, granted Somerset a writ of habeas corpus, and when the hearing began in early 1772, Somerset's advocates argued that the air of England was indeed too pure for slaves to breathe in, for 'the moment [slaves] put their feet on English ground, that moment they become free. They are subject to the laws . . . of this country, and so are their masters, thank God!'[20] After numerous delays, Lord Mansfield gave his judgment, in which he ordered Somerset to be freed, since slavery was indeed illegal under existing English law and could be introduced into England only by positive law. 'No master ever was allowed here to take a slave by force to be sold abroad because he deserted from his service, or for any other reason whatever – therefore the man must be discharged,' pronounced Mansfield. Somerset was accordingly released.[21]

The judgment was widely misunderstood by people who believed that Mansfield had announced the emancipation of all slaves in Britain, but even though this is clearly not what he meant, the case still had far-reaching consequences for black people in Britain, Mary Prince among them. 'I knew that I was free in England,' Prince writes in her *History*, and when she came to England with the Woods in 1828 she accordingly exercised her legal right to remain as a free person. However, she was faced with the difficult choice of freedom in exile or enslavement in Antigua, and in his Supplement Pringle describes how Prince's considerable (and understandable) anxiety to return to her husband conflicted with her reluctance to forfeit her new-found freedom. Prince knew quite well that as soon as she returned to Antigua she would revert to her former slave status, and she was fearful that as a punishment for her recalcitrance she would be put to work as a 'field negro' and forced to work on the plantations rather than in the household, as formerly.

Prince had good reason to be worried about what would happen to her if she returned to Antigua, for the Grace Jones case of 1722 (which Pringle cites in his Supplement) had already set the legal precedent. Like Mary Prince, Grace Jones accompanied her mistress, Mrs Allen, to England from Antigua, but on returning to the Caribbean a few years later she was seized by customs officers as an illegal import. Her 'owner', Mr Allen, subsequently filed for costs and damages, and when the case came to court her supporters argued that Jones was a free British subject who was being unlawfully held in slavery in Antigua. 'The person who is a freeman in *England* returns to slavery in *Antigua*; that is the whole question in this case,' announced Lord Stowell, the judge presiding over the case in the Court of Admiralty, but he eventually decided that Jones was only a free person as long as she remained in England, forfeiting her freedom on returning to Antigua.[22] As Thomas Pringle notes in his Supplement:

[T]he history of Mary Prince furnishes a corollary to Lord Stowell's decision in the case of the slave Grace, and . . . it is most valuable on this account.

Whatever opinions may be held by some readers on the grave question of immediately abolishing Colonial Slavery, nothing assuredly can be more repugnant to the feelings of Englishmen than that the system should be permitted to extend its baneful influence to this country. Yet such is the case, when the slave landed in England still only possesses that qualified degree of freedom, that a change of domicile will determine [i.e. end] it.

Pringle is certainly correct to point out the legal anomaly (and the question of jurisdiction in international law is still a fraught one), but this state of affairs does not seem to have been rectified in Mary Prince's lifetime. Despite having a petition presented to Parliament on her behalf in 1829 in which she pleads 'to return to the *West Indies*, but not as a slave' (see Appendix Two), it does not appear that Prince ever won her legal battle for freedom, and one must assume that she remained in England as a free person, but effectively husband-less and state-less. Clearly, moral air-quality in the early nineteenth century was local rather than international, and slaves were not able to 'breathe' freely anywhere in the world.

SLAVERY AND RELIGION

The law may not have been international in the nineteenth century, but spirituality or religion seemed to provide the enslaved with access to a discourse which apparently transcended the boundaries of 'race' and nation, although Christianity's relationship with enslavement was by no means straightforward, but partly collusive and partly liberatory.[23] While for writers such as Equiano and Gronniosaw, the appropriation of a Christian discourse provided a means of expression, it is also undeniably true that '[t]he Church ... supported the slave trade',[24] according to Eric Williams, historian of the slave trade. All the same, it is also true that a number of the most prominent Abolitionist campaigners in the eighteenth century were Quakers and Methodists, such as William Allen, a leading member of the Quaker movement, who, as Pringle writes in his Supplement, approached the Governor of Antigua to ask him to intervene on Prince's behalf with the Woods, and William Wilberforce, the leading light of the Abolition movement, who began his anti-slavery campaigning only after his religious conversion.[25]

Prince's *History* is, as much as anything, the progress of her movement towards and eventual embracing of Christianity, although her account of her religious conversion is more compressed than that of other black writers (Gronniosaw, Equiano, Marrant), since this text is a political pamphlet rather than a spiritual autobiography. Prince mentions her first attendance at a Methodist meeting on a plantation in Antigua, describing how she subsequently found that her 'spirit' was 'led' to the Moravian church where she was taught to read by 'the Moravian ladies' and where she took Communion for the first time (she says that she was baptized in the English church before this in 1817, but stopped attending because she required written permission from her master. The Anglican church also refused to marry slaves).

The Moravians were descended from the Unitas Fratrum or Church of the Bohemian Brethren, founded in 1457 by a group of Hussites and suppressed in Bohemia and Moravia in the 1620s. In 1722 three men left Moravia and established a settlement in Saxony, Upper Lusitania, and among them was Count Nikolaus von Zinzendorf, who was the leader of the Moravian church at this time. The first Moravian congregations were established in England in 1642, and in 1738 the cross-fertilization of German pietism and High Church Anglicanism 'strangely warmed' John Wesley's heart, although by 1740 he had fallen out with the Moravians over matters of theological dispute. A twentieth-century historian of the Moravian church writes of their '[d]isproportionately extensive overseas missions',[26] describing how, from the 1730s onwards, the Moravians had missionaries stationed in Ceylon (now Sri Lanka), South Africa, Latin America, the Caribbean, North America and Greenland, as well as being well established in Europe, from Denmark to Switzerland, from the Netherlands to the Baltic islands.[27] Zinzendorf himself visited the Caribbean, and as Podmore claims, one of the church's strengths was the way it managed to foster a feeling of international community: 'In the 1740s no other Protestant church in England could offer to anything like the same extent this feeling of being part of a single international organization or the opportunity to hear from fellow-members all over the world, for this was the first international Protestant Church'.[28] Although the Moravian church had been discredited by 1753 (Zinzendorf had run up huge debts, and he left England after being rescued from debtors' prison) it re-established itself towards the end of the century, and in the early nineteenth century it was clearly still a strong force in the colonies.

'Mrs Flanighan', the author of a contemporary description of Antigua,[29] gives a detailed description of the Moravian mission on the island at this time. According to Flanighan, Count Zinzendorf visited Denmark in 1731 where he met a black man, Anthony, who told him about the 'moral darkness' of the West Indies, inspiring Zinzendorf to spread the Moravian word to this part of the world. The first Moravian settlement was established in Antigua in 1756, and the Spring Gardens chapel at St John's which Prince mentions in her *History* was built in 1761. In 1787, 5,465 people were admitted to three church settlements in Antigua, and by 1842 this number had increased to approximately 11,000 members. Flanighan admires the Antiguan Moravians for their 'open-heartedness [and] patriarchal simplicity'. '[A]mong themselves they are ever kind and courteous,' she comments, 'forming, as it were, one large family of affectionate brothers and sisters. They have done much good among the black race, for whose welfare the mission was particularly intended'.[30] However, as Eric Williams notes, Moravian missionaries 'held slaves without hesitation',[31] although they were surely not unique in this respect among religious groups.

Whatever the rights and wrongs of the missionary ideology and its supporters, the Moravian church seems to have given Prince a sense of strength in community and it was here also that she resumed her interrupted education. She tells us that she would not accept Daniel James's proposal of marriage until he had joined the Moravians, and she also comments that the steward in charge of the ship which took her to England two years later was in the same class as her husband at the Moravian church in Antigua, and accordingly treated Prince with kindness during the voyage. When Prince decided to leave the Woods, she turned to the Moravians in Hatton Garden in the first instance. 'The missionaries were very kind to me,' she remarks. '[T]hey were sorry for my destitute situation . . . They were very good people, and they told me to come to the church.' Like Equiano *et al.*, Prince finds a kind of liberation, or at the very least relief, through religion, which provided her and her literary forbears with a means of sanctioned (and perhaps sanctified) insurrection. But it was the Anti-Slavery Society rather than religion which gave her a legal and practical outlet for her protest.

THE ANTI-SLAVERY SOCIETY AND THOMAS PRINGLE

The Committee for the Abolition of the Slave Trade was formed in 1787 by William Wilberforce. However, by 1823 its largely Quaker members decided that a different approach was required after the 1807 Act of Parliament ending the slave trade, and so they established the Anti-Slavery Society. Its leading members included William Wilberforce, Thomas Clarkson, Zachary Macaulay and James Stephen the Elder, and it aimed to persuade the government to adopt their plan for the gradual emancipation of slaves in the British colonies. Pringle's Supplement mentions 'the Anti-Slavery Committee', and presumably by this he is referring to the Agency Committee, formed in 1831 by younger, more radical members of the Anti-Slavery Society. According to historian Reginald Coupland, the committee was '[m]ainly run by George Stephen and three Quakers, Emmanuel and Joseph Cooper and Joseph Sturge, and mainly financed by Quaker money, it employed "agents", paid and unpaid, whom it briefed with the Abolition case and sent to lecture all over the country'.[32]

By the time Mary Prince approached the Anti-Slavery Society in 1828, Thomas Pringle, a Scottish poet who had become involved in the Abolition movement after his return from six years' residence in South Africa, had been secretary for a year. Pringle had gone to South Africa in 1820 where, after working as a librarian, he set up an academy with his friend Fairbairn, with whom he also published a newspaper and magazine. In fact, Pringle gained a reputation as a radical as editor of the *South African Journal*, a short-lived publication which was suppressed by the governor of the colony because it was deemed libellous and seditious, even though it avoided dealing with contentious issues such as slavery and the condition of the Aborigines. Pringle and Fairbairn declared their refusal 'to compromise [their] birth-right as British subjects by editing any publication under a censorship',[33] and Pringle returned to England in October 1826.

On returning to England, Pringle's experiences in South Africa led him to take up the cause of the oppressed African, and an article in the *New Monthly Magazine* in October 1826 on the South African slave trade brought him into Abolitionist circles (a similar article appeared in the *Anti-Slavery Monthly Reporter* on 31 January 1827 – see Appendix Four) and eventually led to his appointment as secretary of the Anti-Slavery Society in 1827. *African Sketches*, a book of verse and prose published in 1834, is self-avowedly 'strictly subsidiary to the same cause' (that is, Abolition), and it features poetic descriptions of a slave market, the massacre and subjugation of native peoples, and a sonnet entitled 'Slavery' (see Appendix One). The autobiographical *Narrative of a Residence in South Africa* (1835) also demonstrates those sympathies which made him an appropriate secretary of the Anti-Slavery Society. Although there was no official slavery at the Cape, Pringle was disgusted at the treatment of the 'Hottentots', who were 'reduced to a state of the most degrading thraldom, in several respects even more wretched than negro slavery itself'.[34] Pringle was certainly no friend of the Boers and he wrote with palpable outrage against their tyranny, condemning what he called 'the frightful perversion of moral sentiment in the dominant class by the uncontrolled exercise of arbitrary power, and the deplorable condition of the natives who lay prostrate under their feet'. In his *Narrative*, Pringle also protests against the inhumanities of South African slavery:

The Native Tribes ... are ready to throw themselves into our arms. Let us open our arms cordially to embrace a new and nobler career of conquest. Let us subdue savage Africa by JUSTICE, by KINDNESS, by the talisman of CHRISTIAN TRUTH. Let US *thus* go forth, in the name and under the blessing of God, gradually to extend the moral influence, and, if it be thought desirable, the territorial boundary also of our Colony, until it shall become an Empire.[35]

Evidently Pringle was not averse to conquest and imperialism as long as they were Christian and humane, and although he was not a missionary Evangelical, he clearly thought that spreading the Gospel among the 'heathen' of Africa would be to their benefit. Perhaps the details of Mary Prince's conversion to Christianity appealed to him, but whatever the reason, he evidently embraced her cause very warmly, campaigning vigorously on her behalf by writing letters to inhabitants of Antigua who might corroborate her claims, employing Prince as a domestic servant in his household when she fell on hard times, presenting a petition to Parliament in 1829 and fighting two separate libel cases against the publisher Thomas Cadell and Prince's owner John Wood in 1833. The energies Pringle exerted on Prince's behalf were not unprecedented: on another occasion he paid a total of £80 to procure the freedom of the slave Nancy Morgan and her son, money that he obtained from the Birmingham Female Society.[36] It could certainly have done Prince's cause no harm that she had such a powerful advocate to back her, and in his Supplement Pringle relates how he used his contacts among the Moravians and the Quakers on her behalf. Like the Abolitionist activist Granville Sharp, who was similarly assiduous in his efforts on behalf of the 'distressed Negro', Pringle seems to have done everything in his power to secure Prince's freedom, but his efforts were thwarted by the anomalies of colonial law and the spite of the Woods, who persisted in refusing to grant Prince the manumission she so desired.

THE *HISTORY* AS PROPAGANDA

I have already argued that the *History* is not a conventional autobiography, and although there are points of thematic contact between Prince's text and those of her black contemporaries and forbears, there are also a number of formal differences. Unlike Olaudah Equiano, who describes his *Narrative* as a memoir,[37] Prince does not have the opportunity to develop an authorial persona or voice in her text, which, as we have seen, is relayed to the reader via an editor and an amanuensis, making it less personal and idiosyncratic. But perhaps this also means that it is a more effective political tool, and in this respect the *History* is strikingly similar to the *Anti-Slavery Monthly Reporter*. The common publication of local Anti-Slavery Society outlets in Great Britain, the *Anti-Slavery Monthly Reporter* was edited by Zachary Macaulay and produced by Pringle, George Stephen and others, and it included accounts of regional Anti-Slavery Society meetings, as well as surveys of the literature of opposition parties. Most importantly, it documented accounts of the abuses inflicted upon slaves in the colonies; graphic and harrowing accounts which were undoubtedly intended to provoke the reader to a sense of outrage and anti-slavery crusading zeal. In his Supplement to the *History*, Pringle lists a number of the cases published in the *Reporter*, drawing attention to the parallels between Prince's experiences and those of other enslaved men and women in Guyana, the Bahamas and Jamaica. These reports usually detail the harsh punishment of slaves who have committed petty crimes, or no crimes at all. The cases cited by Pringle include that of the Jamaican Henry Williams who was flogged until he was nearly dead for preferring the Methodist church to the Anglican; Eleanor Mead who was whipped fifty-eight times merely because her mistress '[took] offence at something which this slave had said or done'; and Kitty Hylton of Jamaica who was brutally beaten for killing a turkey for her master's dinner.[38] The punishments suffered by Prince were no less harsh and unprovoked, and they are described in a similarly impassive style. For example, her second owners in Bermuda, Captain I— and his wife, seem to have ill-treated the black workers in their household at every available opportunity as a matter of course, whipping and pinching and beating them. 'I have seen their flesh ragged and raw with licks [beatings],' Prince says of Cyrus and Jack, the 'two little slave boys' in the I— household who seem to have come in for most punishment. 'Lick – lick – they were never secure one moment from a blow, and their lives were passed in continual fear. My mistress was not contented with using the whip, but often pinched their cheeks and arms in the most cruel manner.' Soon, Prince tells us, her mistress's anger was transferred to her, and she is subjected to violent punishment even though she has committed no crime. 'To strip me naked – to hang me up by the wrists and lay my flesh open with the cow-skin, was an ordinary punishment for even a slight offence,' she writes. Psychological torment was another tactic used by Mrs I—, who would keep Prince awake picking cotton at a bench all night long.

The story of Hetty, Prince's fellow-slave at Captain I—'s, is as harrowing as any of the accounts in the *Anti-Slavery Monthly Reporter*. 'Poor Hetty' as Prince touchingly calls her, was pregnant, and although she was probably carrying Captain I—'s child, this did not stop him whipping her almost to death because a cow had broken loose. After a miscarriage brought on by this horrific beating, Hetty appears to have died of a dropsy (an accumulation of watery fluid in the bodily tissues) and the other workers were unanimous in agreeing that death 'was a good thing for poor Hetty', a clear enough indictment of life on the I—s' estate. Obviously part of the motivation behind publishing the *History* was to publicize atrocities such as these, and in this sense Prince's text served exactly the same function as the *Anti-Slavery Monthly Reporter*. 'Oh the horrors of slavery!' Prince declares after giving an account of yet another brutal beating which she witnessed, this time on the Turks Islands at the hands of her violent master, Mr D—:

How the thought of it pains my heart! But the truth ought to be told of it; and what my eyes have seen I think it is my duty to relate; for few people in England know what slavery is. I have been a slave – I have felt what a slave feels, and I know what a slave knows; and I would have all the good people in England to know it too, that they may break our chains, and set us free.

The aim here is simple enough – by describing the horrors of slavery at first hand, Prince and Pringle hoped to enlist the support of readers whose moral sensibilities would revolt against the crimes that were being committed in the colonies in the name of empire and economics; for this reason Prince takes every possible opportunity to describe the cruelty and violence of the 'Buckra' men and women, as she calls the white people who tormented her. The agonies of the slave market in Bermuda where the words of the white buyers 'fell like cayenne on the fresh wounds of our hearts'; the fierce blows she suffered from Captain I— and Mr D—; the senseless destruction by white people of a makeshift church erected by slaves on the Turks Islands; the night Prince spent locked in the cage (a prison) as a punishment; and the flogging she received by order of the magistrate in Antigua – all these harsh realities are vividly described so that the reader is left in no doubt as to the 'horrors of slavery'. Unlike Olaudah Equiano or Ignatius Sancho, Prince has a clear agenda to fulfil in her *History*, for the former combines the popular forms of travel narrative, spiritual autobiography and protest literature in his *Interesting Narrative* and Sancho's letters are only indirectly political, as he himself had no first-hand experience of enslavement. Prince's narrative, on the other hand, was marketed as a piece of propaganda. At the sixth Annual Meeting of the Birmingham Female Society for the Relief of British Negro Slaves, 'the narrative of Mary Prince was recommenced for purchase ... to every Lady present', and the Society donated £5 'to originate a Fund for the support of Mary Prince'.[39] Martha Pringle's letter corroborating the narrative (reprinted in this edition) was also read aloud to the Society.[40] In this context at least, Prince's narrative was used as evidence of 'the foul reproach and deep sin of African slavery' and it was used as a tool in the continuing campaign for the abolition of enslavement in the colonies.

THE *HISTORY* AND LIBEL CASES

Although there do not seem to have been any contemporary reviews of Prince's *History*, it obviously served its political purpose, for it ran to three editions in the year of its publication and the claims Prince made in her narrative were contentious enough to provoke two libel cases in 1833. The first, in February of that year, was brought by Pringle against Thomas Cadell, who was the publisher of James McQueen's article in *Blackwood's Magazine*. In this article, entitled 'The Colonial Empire of Great Britain', McQueen defended the colonists and asserted the importance of Britain's economic 'possessions' in the Caribbean, exposing what he called 'the venomous Anti-Colonial

Manifesto' as propagated by campaigners such as Pringle and Joseph Phillips, whom he attacks elsewhere. McQueen refutes the veracity of Prince's *History*, claiming that she rejected the Woods' kindness, behaving worse and worse 'until we find her planted in Pringle's family and at his washing tub. From it she was frequently called to his closet to give a narrative of the severities inflicted upon her by several owners, but more especially by her last owners, Mr and Mrs Wood'.[41] Clearly, McQueen believed that Prince was manipulated by the Pringles and the Anti-Slavery Society, an opinion he states very clearly: 'By tools like *Mary Prince* and *Joseph Phillips*, PRINGLE, and the band of which Pringle is the tool and the organ, irritate this country, browbeat the Government, and trample upon, as they are permitted to trample upon, our most important transmarine possessions.'[42]

Pringle sued the publisher Cadell for libel, and the case is reported in *The Times*, 22 February 1833. Prince was called to give evidence, and the newspaper supplies the following description of her, the only one we have: 'She is a negress of very ordinary features, and appeared to be about 35 years of age.' In the end, Prince simply confirmed that she had given an account of her life to Pringle (apparently no further cross-examination was required) and the jury returned a verdict for the plaintiff. Cadell was ordered to pay damages of £5.

Less than a fortnight later, Pringle was back in court, but this time it was his turn to be sued, as Wood had decided to bring a libel action against him. The case is also reported in *The Times*, 1 March 1833 (see Appendix Three), and it gives us a fascinating insight into the details of Prince's life which were withheld by Susanna Strickland and members of the Anti-Slavery Society. At the trial numerous witnesses for Wood refuted the claims that Prince made in her 'pamphlet' as the *History* is called here, asserting that the Woods were always kind and caring to Prince and describing her as lazy and fractious. This time Prince herself took to the witness stand, and although she corroborated the story of ill-treatment and cruelty detailed in the *History*, she was also more frank about her sexual relations. According to Prince's testimony in court, she lived with Captain Abbot for seven years before she was married, and she describes her violent reaction on finding him in bed with 'another woman', adding that because of her relationship with Captain Abbot she 'discharged herself' from the Moravian Society, and she was banned from classes for seven weeks. Evidently she returned to the Moravians, since it is there that she eventually met her husband Daniel James.

Prince's courtroom evidence provides us with important details that were excluded from her *History*, and it also highlights the instability of this text, which has clearly been 'doctored' by zealous anti-slavery campaigners. However, her testimony does not seem to have helped Pringle's cause: this time the verdict was against him and he was ordered to pay damages of £25.

THE *HISTORY* AS PROTEST

Mary Prince's *History* is, then, a piece of propaganda, a protest designed to convince the English reader that the iniquities of slavery in the colonies continued even though an Act of Parliament ending the slave trade had been passed in 1807. The details included in the narrative must have been peculiarly discomforting for the nineteenth-century reader who may have preferred to continue taking her/his coffee, tea and sugar without thinking too deeply about the conditions in which these commodities were produced. Mary Prince's indomitable spirit may also have provided a role model for readers who, in opposing slavery, would not encounter even a modicum of the personal risks she ran in resisting a succession of cruel masters and mistresses. Far from passively accepting the punishments meted out to her, Mary Prince protested against her treatment at every available opportunity, and her *History* is a continuation of this protest. There are numerous examples of Prince's insurrection: on returning to Captain I—, having run away after a particularly savage beating, Prince and her father both told the cruel 'owner' that his behaviour was unacceptable and inhumane. Later, she protected Mr D—'s daughter against her drunken father, announcing with great dignity that 'this [Bermuda] is not Turk's Island'. Nor did she submit to D—'s sexual whims without protest, but after two more beatings she ran away again, telling him that he was 'a very indecent man – very spiteful, and too indecent;

with no shame for his servants, no shame for his own flesh'. Again, she was forced to return, as there was no other place for her to go. While she was owned by the Woods, Prince took in washing and sold provisions until she had managed to scrape together the $100 she needed to buy her own freedom, but she was thwarted by the Woods' refusal to sell her. When Prince married Daniel James, she did not even bother to gain the Woods' permission, another indication of her spirit and her refusal to accept her slave status. Her independence is again in evidence on coming to London, where the Woods' continuing cruelty eventually drove her to assert her legal right to remain in England as a free woman. 'To be free is very sweet,' she had told Mrs Wood earlier, but it is a sweetness which is not unalloyed with bitterness, since, as we have seen, Prince's freedom was gained at the expense of her emotional happiness. Although she was fully aware of the risks she ran on leaving the Woods' household in London, Prince did so in characteristically outspoken style:

I am going out of this house as I was ordered; but I have done no wrong at all to my owners, neither here nor in the West Indies. I always worked very hard to please them, both by night and day; but there was no giving satisfaction ... I told my mistress I was sick, and yet she has ordered me out of doors. This is the fourth time; and now I am going out.

This simple and dignified statement shows Prince's clear sense of the injustice she had suffered at the Woods' hands (and, by implication, the hands of all the other masters and mistresses who treated her no better), but she speaks without rancour here. Even in the powerful statement which closes her narrative, it is the evils of slavery in general rather than the cruelty of a particular master or mistress which is the focus of her invective, and from the notable shift in register it appears that Pringle has given Prince free rein to express her anger at this point. 'The whole of this paragraph especially, is given as nearly as was possible in Mary's precise words,' Pringle informs the reader in a footnote, and the section is indeed more colloquial and polemical than the rest of the text. 'We don't mind hard work, if we had proper treatment, and proper wages like English servants ...' Prince states. 'But they won't give it: they will have work – work – work, night and day, sick or well, till we are quite done up; and we must not speak up nor look amiss, however much we be abused.'

Mary Prince's life was certainly blighted by slavery, but from her *History* it does not seem that she was altogether 'done up' by it, unlike some of the other victims of cruelty she describes in the course of her narrative. That she was not broken by the experience is testimony to her resilience and her sense of justice, her refusal to accept that the word of the white woman or man was law when her/his behaviour was so manifestly cruel and unjust. Unlike so many of her companions-in-oppression, Mary Prince survived to tell her own tale, and she speaks consciously and vehemently on behalf of those who, for whatever reason, have no voice. 'I have been a slave myself,' she reminds us towards the end of the *History*. 'I know what slaves feel – I can tell by myself what other slaves feel, and by what they have told me.' Her narrative is not just a record of her personal experiences, it is also a protest on behalf of all those who were forced to suffer the abuse of their human rights during the era of transatlantic slavery.

NOTES

1. Paul Gilroy, *The Black Atlantic. Modernity and Double Consciousness* (London: Verso, 1993), p. ix.
2. Apart from her last owners, Mr and Mrs Wood, the full names of Prince's masters and mistresses are not given in the *History*. Pringle claims that this is to protect surviving relatives, but presumably it is also to prevent libel action. See 'The *History* and Libel Cases' (pp. xxviii–xxx) for the two libel cases in which Pringle was involved after publication of the *History*.
3. Ignatius Sancho, *The Letters of the Late Ignatius Sancho* (London, 1782), ed. Vincent Carretta (New York: Penguin, 1998), pp. 130–31.
4. Henry Louis Gates jun., *Loose Canons. Notes on the Culture Wars* (New York: Oxford University Press, 1992), p. 23.
5. *Ibid.*, 66.
6. Henry Louis Gates jun., Foreword to the Schomburg Library of Nineteenth-Century Black Women Writers, in Phillis Wheatley, *The Collected Works of Phillis Wheatley*, ed. John C. Shields (New York: Oxford University Press, 1988), p. viii.

7. Wheatley, viii–ix.

8. Ukawsaw Gronniosaw, *A Narrative of the Most Remarkable Particulars in the Life of James Albert Ukawsaw Gronniosaw, an African Prince, As Related By Himself* (c. 1770; Leeds, 1810), p. 35.

9. Robert Young, *Colonial Desire. Hybridity in Theory, Culture and Race* (London: Routledge, 1995), pp. 6–7.

10. Edward Long, *The History of Jamaica: or, a General Survey of the Antient and Modern State of that Island*, 3 vols (1774), vol. II, pp. 336, 363.

11. *Ibid.*, III: 475.

12. *Ibid.*, 484, 485.

13. See Peter Fryer, *Staying Power. The History of Black People in Britain* (London: Pluto Press, 1984), p. 152.

14. See Homi K. Bhabha, 'Of Mimicry and Man. The Ambivalence of Colonial Discourse', in *The Location of Culture* (London: Routledge, 1994) pp. 85–92.

15. See James Walvin, *Black and White. The Negro and English Society 1555–1945* (London: Penguin, 1973), p. 46; Folarin Shyllon, *Black People in Britain 1555–1833* (Oxford: Oxford University Press, 1977), p. 4; Fryer, 68.

16. Fryer, 113.

17. James Walvin, *Slaves and Slavery. The British Colonial Experience* (Manchester: Manchester University Press, 1992), p. 34.

18. Fryer, 114.

19. William Blackstone, *Commentaries on the Laws of England*, 4 vols, 16th edn (London, 1825), vol. I, p. 127.

20. Quoted in Fryer, 122.

21. James Walvin, *Black Ivory. A History of British Slavery* (London: Fontana Press, 1993), p. 15.

22. *Reports of Cases Argued and Determined in the High Court of Admiralty*, vol. II (1825–1832), pp. 94–134. See also Fryer, 130–32.

23. Walvin, *Black and White*, 66.

24. Eric Williams, *Capitalism and Slavery* (Chapel Hill: University Press of North Carolina, 1994), pp. 42–4.

25. James Walvin argues that Williams's emphasis on economics in the ending of the slave trade underplays the role of Christian activist movements in the Abolition process (see Walvin, *Slaves and Slavery*, 93–4). See also Reginald Coupland, *The British Anti Slavery Movement* (London: Butterworth, 1933), p. 72.

26. Colin Podmore, *The Moravian Church in England, 1728–1760* (Oxford: Clarendon Press, 1998), p. 1.

27. *Ibid.*, xx.

28. *Ibid.*, 123–4.

29. Mrs Flanighan, *Antigua and the Antiguans: a Full Account of the Colony and Its Inhabitants from the Time of the Caribs to the Present Day*, 2 vols (London, 1844).

30. *Ibid.*, I: 250.

31. Williams, 43.

32. Coupland, 137.

33. Thomas Pringle, *Narrative of a Residence in South Africa*, 2nd edn (London, 1835), p. 322.

34. *Ibid.*, 479.

35. *Ibid.*, 190.

36. Clare Midgley, *Women Against Slavery. The British Campaigns, 1780–1870* (London: Routledge, 1992), p. 87.

37. Olaudah Equiano, *The Interesting Narrative of Olaudah Equiano, or Gustavus Vassa, the African, Written by Himself* (London, 1794), ed. Vincent Carretta (New York: Penguin, 1995), p. 31.

38. *Anti-Slavery Monthly Reporter*, vol. 3. no. 65 (1830), pp. 356–7; vol. 3, no. 64 (1830), pp. 345–7; vol. 4, no. 76 (1831), pp. 140–43.

39. 'Minute Book of the Ladies' Society for the Relief of Negro Slaves 1825–1852', p. 109.

40. *Ibid.*

41. James McQueen, 'The Colonial Empire of Great Britain', in *Blackwood's Edinburgh Magazine*, vol. 30, no. 187 (November 1831), pp. 744–64.

42. *Ibid.*, 752.

FURTHER READING

PRIMARY

Anti-Slavery Monthly Reporter, 5 vols (London, 1827–38).

Blackstone, William, *Commentaries on the Laws of England*, 4 vols. 16th edn (London, 1825).

Cugoano, Ottobah (or John Stuart), *Thoughts and Sentiments of the Evil and Wicked Traffic of Slavery and Commerce of the Human Species* (1787), ed. Vincent Carretta (New York: Penguin, 1999).

Edwards, Bryan, *The History, Civil and Commercial, of the British West Indies*, 5 vols, 5th edn (London, 1819).

Equiano, Olaudah, *The Interesting Narrative of Olaudah Equiano, or Gustavus Vassa, the African, Written by Himself* (London, 1794), ed. Vincent Carretta (New York: Penguin, 1995).

Flanighan, Mrs, *Antigua and the Antiguans; a Full Account of the Colony and Its Inhabitants from the Time of the Caribs to the Present Day*, 2 vols (London, 1844).

Gronniosaw, Albert, *A Narrative of the Most Remarkable Particulars in the Life of James Albert Ukawsaw Gronniosaw, an African Prince, As Related by Himself* (c. 1770; Leeds, 1810).

Long, Edward, *The History of Jamaica: or, a General Survey of the Antient and Modern State of that Island*, 3 vols (London, 1774).

Marrant, John, *A Narrative of the Lord's Wonderful Dealings with John Marrant, a Black*, 2nd edn (London, 1785).

McKinnen, Daniel, *A Tour Through the British West Indies, in the Years 1802 and 1803* (London, 1804).

McQueen, James, 'The Colonial Empire of Great Britain', in *Blackwood's Edinburgh Magazine*, vol. 30, no. 187 (November 1831), pp. 744–64.

Prince, Mary, *The History of Mary Prince, A West Indian Slave. Related By Herself*, ed. Moira Ferguson (London: Pandora, 1987).

Pringle, Thomas, *African Sketches* (London, 1834)
  Narrative of a Residence in South Africa, 2nd edn (London, 1835)
  The Poetical Works of Thomas Pringle, with a Sketch of his Life (London, 1838).

Sancho, Ignatius, *The Letters of the Late Ignatius Sancho* (London, 1782), ed. Vincent Carretta (New York: Penguin, 1998).

Wheatley, Phillis, *The Collected Works of Phillis Wheatley*, ed. John C. Shields (New York: Oxford University Press, 1988).

SECONDARY

Andrews, William L. (ed.), *Six Women's Slave Narratives* (New York: Oxford University Press, 1988).

Bhabha, Homi K., 'Of Mimicry and Man. The Ambivalence of Colonial Discourse', in *The Location of Culture* (London: Routledge, 1994), pp. 85–92.

Bolt, Christine, *The Anti-Slavery Movement and Reconstruction. A Study of Anglo-American Co-operation 1833–77* (Oxford: Oxford University Press, 1969).

Carretta, Vincent, *Unchained Voices. An Anthology of Black Authors in the English-Speaking World of the Eighteenth Century* (Lexington: Kentucky University Press, 1996).

Coupland, Reginald, *The British Anti-Slavery Movement* (London: Butterworth, 1933).

Curtin, Philip, *Africa Remembered. Narratives of West Africans from the Era of the Slave Trade* (Madison: Wisconsin University Press, 1967).

Davis, C. T. and Gates, Henry Louis jun., *The Slave's Narrative* (New York: Oxford University Press, 1985).

Edwards, Paul and Dabydeen, David (eds), *Black Writers in Britain 1760–1890. An Anthology* (Edinburgh: Edinburgh University Press, 1991).

Ferguson, Moira, *Nine Black Women Writers. An Anthology of Nine-*

teenth-Century Writers from the United States, Canada, Bermuda and the Caribbean (London: Routledge, 1998)

    Subject to Others. British Women Writers and Colonial Slavery 1670–1834 (London: Routledge, 1992).

Fleischner, Jennifer, *Mastering Slavery. Memory, Family and Identity in Women's Slave Narratives* (New York: New York University Press, 1996).

Fryer, Peter, *Staying Power. The History of Black People in Britain* (London: Pluto Press, 1984).

Gates, Henry Louis jun., *Loose Canons. Notes on the Culture Wars* (New York: Oxford University Press, 1992)

    The Signifying Monkey. A Theory of African-American Literary Criticism (New York: Oxford University Press, 1988).

Gilroy, Paul, *The Black Atlantic. Modernity and Double Consciousness* (London: Verso, 1993).

Hall, Stuart, 'Cultural Identity and Diaspora', in Jonathan Rutherford (ed.), *Identity, Community, Culture, Difference* (London: Lawrence & Wishart, 1990).

Higman, B. W., *Slave Populations of the British Caribbean 1807–1834* (Baltimore: Johns Hopkins University Press, 1984).

Johnson, Howard, *The Bahamas in Slavery and Freedom* (Kingston, Jamaica: Randle Publishers, 1991).

Midgley, Clare, *Women Against Slavery. The British Campaigns, 1780–1870* (London: Routledge, 1992).

Podmore, Colin, *The Moravian Church in England, 1728–1760* (Oxford: Clarendon Press, 1998).

Potkay, Adam and Burr, Sandar (eds), *Black Atlantic Writers of the Eighteenth Century. Living the New Exodus in England and the Americas* (Basingstoke: Macmillan, 1995).

Roberts, Diane, *The Myth of Aunt Jemima. Representations of Race and Region* (London: Routledge, 1994).

Sandiford, Keith, *Measuring the Moment. Strategies of Protest in Eighteenth-Century Afro-English Writing* (London: Associated University Presses, 1988).

Segal, Ronald, *The Black Diaspora* (London: Faber & Faber, 1995).

Shyllon, Folarin, *Black People in Britain 1555–1833* (Oxford: Oxford University Press, 1977).

Sypher, Wylie, *Guinea's Captive Kings. British Anti-Slavery Literature of the XVIIIth Century* (Chapel Hill: University Press of North Carolina, 1942).

Thomas, Hugh, *The Slave Trade. The History of the Atlantic Slave Trade 1440–1870* (New York: Simon & Schuster, 1997).

Walvin, James, *Black and White. The Negro and English Society 1555–1945* (London: Penguin, 1973)

    Black Ivory. A History of British Slavery (London: Fontana Press, 1993)

    Black Personalities in the Era of the Slave Trade (London: Macmillan, 1993)

    Slaves and Slavery. The British Colonial Experience (Manchester: Manchester University Press, 1992).

Williams, Eric, *Capitalism and Slavery* (Chapel Hill: University Press of North Carolina, 1994).

Young, Robert, *Colonial Desire. Hybridity in Theory, Culture and Race* (London: Routledge, 1995).

CHRONOLOGY

1788	Mary Prince born in Brackish Pond, Bermuda Charles Myners, first owner Bought by Captain Williams and given to Betsey Williams, his grandchild
1800	Hired out to Mrs Pruden at twelve years old Sold to Captain I—, taken to Spanish Point in Bermuda where she remains for five years Sold to Mr D— and sent to the Turks Islands to work in the salt ponds Works for Mr D— for 'several years'; returns to Bermuda where she works for Captain I— again Hired out to work at Cedar Hills, although still 'belongs' to Captain I—
1815	Sold to Mr John Wood who takes her to Antigua
c. 1817	Begins to attend the Moravian church, where she meets her husband, Daniel James, a free carpenter and cooper
Dec. 1826	Prince and James are married at the Moravian Chapel, Spring Gardens, Antigua
1828	Accompanies the Woods to England
Nov. 1828	Mary leaves the Woods after thirteen years of ill-treatment and goes to the Anti-Slavery office in Aldermanbury where she consults George Stephen, a lawyer
1829	Works for Mrs Forsyth as a charwoman

	Goes back to Anti-Slavery Society when she runs out of money
June 1829	Petition presented to Parliament on Prince's behalf
Dec. 1829	Employed by Mr and Mrs Pringle as a domestic servant
1831	Publication of *The History of Mary Prince* which runs to three editions that year Prince is forty-three years old
Feb. 1833	Libel trial, *Pringle* v. *Cadell*, at which Prince takes the witness stand
March 1833	Libel trial, *Wood* v. *Pringle*, at which Prince gives evidence

A NOTE ON THE TEXT

Three editions of *The History of Mary Prince* were published in 1831. Only the first and the third editions are extant, and I have used the latter which contains a very small number of minor changes that have been noted in the text. Other than these changes, the first and the third editions are substantially the same. Original spelling and punctuation have been retained, except for the following: double inverted commas have been replaced by single quotation marks; and full points following headings and the contractions 'Mr', 'Mrs' and 'Dr' have been removed. In addition, the spacing and layout of the text in general has been slightly updated (for example, the dashes constituting names that have been 'erased' – Capt. I—, Mr D— and so on – have been shortened).

My editorial notes to the footnotes follow the usual Notes (and are indicated by superscript letters).

The section of verse quoted The title page from *The History of Mary Prince*, 3rd edn, supplied by Bodleian Library, University of Oxford is from the last two stanzas of William Cowper's 'The Negro's Complaint' (*The Poems of William Cowper*, ed. John Baird and Charles Ryskamp, 3 vols, Oxford: Clarendon Press, 1980–95, vol. III, p. 14).

THE

HISTORY OF MARY PRINCE,

A WEST INDIAN SLAVE.

RELATED BY HERSELF.

———

WITH A SUPPLEMENT BY THE EDITOR.

———

To which is added,

THE NARRATIVE OF ASA-ASA,

A CAPTURED AFRICAN.

———

"By our sufferings, since ye brought us
To the man-degrading mart,—
All sustain'd by patience, taught us
Only by a broken heart,—
Deem our nation brutes no longer,
Till some reason ye shall find
Worthier of regard, and stronger
Than the colour of our kind."   COWPER.

———

THIRD EDITION.

———

LONDON:
PUBLISHED BY F. WESTLEY AND A. H. DAVIS,
STATIONERS' HALL COURT;
AND BY WAUGH & INNES, EDINBURGH:
And supplied at trade price to Anti-Slavery Associations by JOSEPH PHILLIPS,
18, Aldermanbury.
———
1831.

PREFACE

The idea of writing Mary Prince's history was first suggested by herself. She wished it to be done, she said, that good people in England might hear from a slave what a slave had felt and suffered; and a letter of her late master's, which will be found in the Supplement,[1] induced me to accede to her wish without farther delay. The more immediate object of the publication will afterwards appear.

The narrative was taken down from Mary's own lips by a lady[2] who happened to be at the time residing in my family as a visitor. It was written out fully, with all the narrator's repetitions and prolixities, and afterwards pruned into its present shape; retaining, as far as was practicable, Mary's exact expressions and peculiar phraseology. No fact of importance has been omitted, and not a single circumstance or sentiment has been added. It is essentially her own, without any material alteration farther than was requisite to exclude redundancies and gross grammatical errors, so as to render it clearly intelligible.

After it had been thus written out, I went over the whole, carefully examining her on every fact and circumstance detailed; and in all that relates to her residence in Antigua I had the advantage of being assisted in this scrutiny by Mr Joseph Phillips,[3] who was a resident in that colony during the same period, and had known her there.

The names of all the persons mentioned by the narrator have been printed in full, except those of Capt. I— and his wife, and that of Mr D—, to whom conduct of peculiar atrocity is ascribed. These three individuals are now gone to answer at a far more awful tribunal than that of public opinion, for the deeds of which their former bondwoman accuses them; and to hold them up more openly to human reprobation could no longer affect themselves, while it might deeply lacerate the feelings of their surviving and perhaps innocent relatives, without any commensurate public advantage.

Without detaining the reader with remarks on other points, which will be adverted to more conveniently in the Supplement, I shall here merely notice farther, that the Anti-Slavery Society[4] have no concern whatever with this publication, nor are they in any degree responsible for the statements it contains. I have published the tract, not as their Secretary, but in my private capacity; and any profits that may arise from the sale will be exclusively appropriated to the benefit of Mary Prince herself.

While Mary's history was in the press, I was furnished by my friend Mr George Stephen[5] with the interesting narrative of Asa-Asa,[6] a captured African now under his protection, and have printed it as a suitable appendix.

THO. PRINGLE[7]

London, January 25, 1831.

POSTSCRIPT – Second Edition[8]

Since the First Edition of this Tract was published, Mary Prince has been afflicted with a disease in the eyes, which, it is feared, may terminate in total blindness: such, at least, is the apprehension of some skilful medical gentlemen who have been consulted on the case. Should this unfortunately be the result, the condition of the poor negro woman, thus cruelly and hopelessly severed from her husband and her home, will be one peculiarly deserving of commiseration; and I mention the circumstance at present on purpose to induce the friends of humanity to promote the more zealously the sale of this publication, with a view to provide a little fund for her future benefit. Whatever be the subsequent lot that Providence may have in reserve for her, the seasonable sympathy thus manifested in her behalf, will neither be fruitlessly expended nor unthankfully received; while, in accordance with the benign Scripture mandate, it will serve to mitigate and relieve, as far as human kindness can, the afflictions of 'the stranger and the exile who is in our land within our gates.'[9]

T.P.

March 22, 1831.

* * * *The present Cheap Edition, price* 1s. *for single copies, and* 6d. *each, if* 25 *or more are ordered, is printed expressly to facilitate the circulation of this Tract by Anti-Slavery Societies.*

HISTORY OF MARY PRINCE,

A WEST INDIAN SLAVE

(Related by herself)

I WAS born at Brackish-Pond, in Bermuda,[10] on a farm belonging to Mr Charles Myners. My mother was a household slave; and my father, whose name was Prince, was a sawyer belonging to Mr Trimmingham, a ship-builder at Crow-Lane.[11] When I was an infant, old Mr Myners died, and there was a division of the slaves and other property among the family. I was bought along with my mother by old Captain Darrel, and given to his grandchild, little Miss Betsey Williams. Captain Williams, Mr Darrel's son-in-law, was master of a vessel which traded to several places in America and the West Indies, and he was seldom at home long together.

Mrs Williams was a kind-hearted good woman, and she treated all her slaves well. She had only one daughter, Miss Betsey, for whom I was purchased, and who was about my own age. I was made quite a pet of by Miss Betsey, and loved her very much. She used to lead me about by the hand, and call me her little nigger. This was the happiest period of my life; for I was too young to understand rightly my condition as a slave, and too thoughtless and full of spirits to look forward to the days of toil and sorrow.

My mother was a household slave[12] in the same family. I was under her own care, and my little brothers and sisters were my play-fellows and companions. My mother had several fine children after she came to Mrs Williams, – three girls and two boys The tasks given out to us children were light, and we used to play together with Miss Betsey, with as much freedom almost as if she had been our sister.

My master, however, was a very harsh, selfish man; and we always dreaded his return from sea. His wife was herself much afraid of him;

and, during his stay at home, seldom dared to shew her usual kindness to the slaves. He often left her, in the most distressed circumstances, to reside in other female society, at some place in the West Indies of which I have forgot the name. My poor mistress bore his ill-treatment with great patience, and all her slaves loved and pitied her. I was truly attached to her, and, next to my own mother, loved her better than any creature in the world. My obedience to her commands was cheerfully given: it sprung solely from the affection I felt for her, and not from fear of the power which the white people's law had given her over me.

I had scarcely reached my twelfth year when my mistress became too poor to keep so many of us at home; and she hired me out to Mrs Pruden, a lady who lived about five miles off, in the adjoining parish,[13] in a large house near the sea. I cried bitterly at parting with my dear mistress and Miss Betsey, and when I kissed my mother and brothers and sisters, I thought my young heart would break, it pained me so. But there was no help; I was forced to go. Good Mrs Williams comforted me by saying that I should still be near the home I was about to quit, and might come over and see her and my kindred whenever I could obtain leave of absence from Mrs Pruden. A few hours after this I was taken to a strange house, and found myself among strange people. This separation seemed a sore trial to me then; but oh! 'twas light, light to the trials I have since endured! – 'twas nothing – nothing to be mentioned with them; but I was a child then, and it was according to my strength.[14]

I knew that Mrs Williams could no longer maintain me; that she was fain to part with me for my food and clothing; and I tried to submit myself to the change. My new mistress was a passionate woman; but yet she did not treat me very unkindly. I do not remember her striking me but once, and that was for going to see Mrs Williams when I heard she was sick, and staying longer than she had given me leave to do. All my employment at this time was nursing a sweet baby, little Master Daniel; and I grew so fond of my nursling that it was my greatest delight to walk out with him by the sea-shore, accompanied by his brother and sister, Miss Fanny and Master James. – Dear Miss Fanny! She was a sweet, kind young lady, and so fond of me that she wished me to learn all that she knew herself; and her method of teaching me was as follows: – Directly she had said her lessons to her grandmamma, she used to come running to me, and make me repeat them one by one after her; and in a few months I was able not only to say my letters but to spell many small words. But this happy state was not to last long. Those days were too pleasant to last. My heart always softens when I think of them.

At this time Mrs Williams died. I was told suddenly of her death, and my grief was so great that, forgetting I had the baby in my arms, I ran away directly to my poor mistress's house; but reached it only in time to see the corpse carried out. Oh, that was a day of sorrow, – a heavy day! All the slaves cried. My mother cried and lamented her sore; and I (foolish creature!) vainly entreated them to bring my dear mistress back to life. I knew nothing rightly about death then, and it seemed a hard thing to bear. When I thought about my mistress I felt as if the world was all gone wrong; and for many days and weeks I could think of nothing else. I returned to Mrs Pruden's; but my sorrow was too great to be comforted, for my own dear mistress was always in my mind. Whether in the house or abroad, my thoughts were always talking to me about her.

I staid at Mrs Pruden's about three months after this; I was then sent back to Mr Williams to be sold. Oh, that was a sad sad time! I recollect the day well. Mrs Pruden came to me and said, 'Mary, you will have to go home directly; your master is going to be married, and he means to sell you and two of your sisters to raise money for the wedding.' Hearing this I burst out a crying, – though I was then far from being sensible of the full weight of my misfortune, or of the misery that waited for me. Besides, I did not like to leave Mrs Pruden, and the dear baby, who had grown very fond of me. For some time I could scarcely believe that Mrs Pruden was in earnest, till I received orders for my immediate return. – Dear Miss Fanny! how she cried at parting with me, whilst I kissed and hugged the baby, thinking I should never see him again. I left Mrs Pruden's, and walked home with a heart full of sorrow. The idea of being sold away from my mother and Miss Betsey was so frightful, that I dared not trust myself to think about it. We had been bought of Mr Myners, as I have mentioned, by Miss Betsey's grandfather, and given to her, so that we were by right *her* property, and I never thought we should be separated or sold away from her.

When I reached the house, I went in directly to Miss Betsey. I found her in great distress; and she cried out as soon as she saw me, 'Oh, Mary! my father is going to sell you all to raise money to marry that wicked woman. You are *my* slaves, and he has no right to sell you; but it is all to please her.' She then told me that my mother was living with her father's sister at a house close by, and I went there to see her. It was a sorrowful meeting; and we lamented with a great and sore crying our unfortunate situation. 'Here comes one of my poor picaninnies!'[15] she said, the moment I came in, 'one of the poor slave-brood who are to be sold to-morrow.'

Oh dear! I cannot bear to think of that day, – it is too much. – It recalls the great grief that filled my heart, and the woeful thoughts that passed to and fro through my mind, whilst listening to the pitiful words of my poor mother, weeping for the loss of her children. I wish I could find words to tell you all I then felt and suffered. The great God above alone knows the thoughts of the poor slave's heart, and the bitter pains which follow such separations as these. All that we love taken away from us – Oh, it is sad, sad! and sore to be borne! – I got no sleep that night for thinking of the morrow; and dear Miss Betsey was scarcely less distressed. She could not bear to part with her old playmates, and she cried sore and would not be pacified.

The black morning at length came; it came too soon for my poor mother and us. Whilst she was putting on us the new osnaburgs[16] in which we were to be sold, she said, in a sorrowful voice, (I shall never forget it!) 'See, I am *shrouding* my poor children; what a task for a mother!' – She then called Miss Betsey to take leave of us. 'I am going to carry my little chickens to market,' (these were her very words,) 'take your last look of them; may be you will see them no more.' 'Oh, my poor slaves! my own slaves!' said dear Miss Betsey, 'you belong to me; and it grieves my heart to part with you.' – Miss Betsey kissed us all, and, when she left us, my mother called the rest of the slaves to bid us good bye. One of them, a woman named Moll, came with her infant in her arms. 'Ah!' said my mother, seeing her turn away and look at her child with the tears in her eyes, 'your turn will come next.' The slaves could say nothing to comfort us; they could only weep and lament with us. When I left my dear little brothers and the house in which I had been brought up, I thought my heart would burst.

Our mother, weeping as she went, called me away with the children Hannah and Dinah, and we took the road that led to Hamble Town,[17] which we reached about four o'clock in the afternoon. We followed my mother to the market-place, where she placed us in a row against a large house, with our backs to the wall and our arms folded across our breasts. I, as the eldest, stood first, Hannah next to me, then Dinah; and our mother stood beside, crying over us. My heart throbbed with grief and terror so violently, that I pressed my hands quite tightly across my breast, but I could not keep it still, and it continued to leap as though it would burst out of my body. But who cared for that? Did one of the many by-standers, who were looking at us so carelessly, think of the pain that wrung the hearts of the negro woman and her young ones? No, no! They were not all bad, I dare say, but slavery hardens white people's hearts towards the blacks; and many of them were not slow to make their remarks upon us aloud, without regard to our grief – though their light words fell like cayenne[18] on the fresh wounds of our hearts. Oh those white people have small hearts who can only feel for themselves.

At length the vendue master,[19] who was to offer us for sale like sheep or cattle, arrived, and asked my mother which was the eldest. She said nothing, but pointed to me. He took me by the hand, and led me out into the middle of the street, and, turning me slowly round, exposed me to the view of those who attended the vendue. I was soon surrounded by strange men, who examined and handled me in the same manner that a butcher would a calf or a lamb he was about to purchase, and who talked about my shape and size in like words – as if I could no more understand their meaning than the dumb beasts. I was then put up to sale. The bidding commenced at a few pounds, and gradually rose to fifty-seven,* when I was knocked down to the

* Bermuda currency; about £38 sterling.

highest bidder; and the people who stood by said that I had fetched a great sum for so young a slave.

I then saw my sisters led forth, and sold to different owners; so that we had not the sad satisfaction of being partners in bondage. When the sale was over, my mother hugged and kissed us, and mourned over us, begging of us to keep up a good heart, and do our duty to our new masters. It was a sad parting; one went one way, one another, and our poor mammy went home with nothing.*

My new master was a Captain I——, who lived at Spanish Point.[20] After parting with my mother and sisters, I followed him to his store, and he gave me into the charge of his son, a lad about my own age, Master Benjy, who took me to my new home. I did not know where I was going, or what my new master would do with me. My heart was quite broken with grief, and my thoughts went back continually

* Let the reader compare the above affecting account, taken down from the mouth of this negro woman, with the following description of a vendue of slaves at the Cape of Good Hope, published by me in 1826,[a] from the letter of a friend, – and mark their similarity in several characteristic circumstances. The resemblance is easily accounted for: slavery wherever it prevails produces similar effects. – 'Having heard that there was to be a sale of cattle, farm stock, &c. by auction, at a Veld-Cornet's[b] in the vicinity, we halted our waggon one day for the purpose of procuring a fresh spann of oxen. Among the stock of the farm sold, was a female slave and her three children. The two eldest children were girls, the one about thirteen years of age, and the other about eleven; the youngest was a boy. The whole family were exhibited together, but they were sold separately, and to different purchasers. The farmers examined them as if they had been so many head of cattle. While the sale was going on, the mother and her children were exhibited on a table, that they might be seen by the company, which was very large. There could not have been a finer subject for an able painter than this unhappy group. The tears, the anxiety, the anguish of the mother, while she met the gaze of the multitude, eyed the different countenances of the bidders, or cast a heart-rending look upon the children; and the simplicity and touching sorrow of the young ones, while they clung to their distracted parent, wiping their eyes, and half concealing their faces, – contrasted with the marked insensibility and jocular countenances of the spectators and purchasers, – furnished a striking commentary on the miseries of slavery, and its debasing effects upon the hearts of its abettors. While the woman was in this distressed situation she was asked, "Can you feed sheep?" Her reply was so indistinct that it escaped me; but it was probably in the negative, for her purchaser rejoined, in a loud and harsh voice, "Then I will teach you with the sjamboc," (a whip made of the rhinoceros' hide.) The mother and her three children were sold to three separate purchasers; and they were literally torn from each other.' – Ed.

to those from whom I had been so suddenly parted. 'Oh, my mother! my mother!' I kept saying to myself, 'Oh, my mammy and my sisters and my brothers, shall I never see you again!'

Oh, the trials! the trials! they make the salt water come into my eyes when I think of the days in which I was afflicted – the times that are gone; when I mourned and grieved with a young heart for those whom I loved.

It was night when I reached my new home. The house was large, and built at the bottom of a very high hill; but I could not see much of it that night. I saw too much of it afterwards. The stones and the timber were the best things in it; they were not so hard as the hearts of the owners.*

Before I entered the house, two slave women, hired from another owner, who were at work in the yard, spoke to me, and asked who I belonged to? I replied, 'I am come to live here.' 'Poor child, poor child!' they both said; 'you must keep a good heart, if you are to live here.' – When I went in, I stood up crying in a corner. Mrs I— came and took off my hat, a little black silk hat Miss Pruden made for me, and said in a rough voice, 'You are not come here to stand up in corners and cry, you are come here to work.' She then put a child into my arms, and, tired as I was, I was forced instantly to take up my old occupation of a nurse. – I could not bear to look at my mistress, her countenance was so stern. She was a stout tall woman with a very dark complexion, and her brows were always drawn together into a frown. I thought of the words of the two slave women when I saw Mrs I—, and heard the harsh sound of her voice.

The person I took the most notice of that night was a French Black[21] called Hetty, whom my master took in privateering[22] from another vessel, and made his slave. She was the most active woman I ever saw, and she was tasked to her utmost. A few minutes after my arrival she came in from milking the cows, and put the sweet-potatoes on for supper. She then fetched home the sheep, and penned them in the fold; drove home the cattle, and staked them about the pond

* These strong expressions, and all of a similar character in this little narrative, are given verbatim as uttered by Mary Prince. – *Ed.*

side;* fed and rubbed down my master's horse, and gave the hog and the fed cow† their suppers; prepared the beds, and undressed the children, and laid them to sleep. I liked to look at her and watch all her doings, for her's was the only friendly face I had as yet seen, and I felt glad that she was there. She gave me my supper of potatoes and milk, and a blanket to sleep upon, which she spread for me in the passage before the door of Mrs I—'s chamber.

I got a sad fright, that night. I was just going to sleep, when I heard a noise in my mistress's room; and she presently called out to inquire if some work was finished that she had ordered Hetty to do. 'No, Ma'am, not yet,' was Hetty's answer from below. On hearing this, my master started up from his bed, and just as he was, in his shirt, ran down stairs with a long cow-skin‡ in his hand. I heard immediately after, the cracking of the thong, and the house rang to the shrieks of poor Hetty, who kept crying out, 'Oh, Massa! Massa! me dead. Massa! have mercy upon me – don't kill me outright.' – This was a sad beginning for me. I sat up upon my blanket, trembling with terror, like a frightened hound, and thinking that my turn would come next. At length the house became still, and I forget for a little while all my sorrows by falling fast asleep.

The next morning my mistress set about instructing me in my tasks. She taught me to do all sorts of household work; to wash and bake, pick cotton and wool, and wash floors, and cook. And she taught me (how can I ever forget it!) more things than these; she caused me to know the exact difference between the smart of the rope, the cart-whip, and the cow-skin, when applied to my naked body by her own cruel hand. And there was scarcely any punishment more dreadful than the blows I received on my face and head from her hard heavy fist. She was a fearful woman, and a savage mistress to her slaves.

There were two little slave boys in the house, on whom she vented her bad temper in a special manner. One of these children was a mulatto, called Cyrus,[23] who had been bought while an infant in his

---

* The cattle on a small plantation in Bermuda are, it seems, often thus staked or tethered, both night and day, in situations where grass abounds.
† A cow fed for slaughter.
‡ A thong of hard twisted hide, known by this name in the West Indies.

mother's arms; the other, Jack, was an African from the coast of Guinea,[24] whom a sailor had given or sold to my master. Seldom a day passed without these boys receiving the most severe treatment, and often for no fault at all. Both my master and mistress seemed to think that they had a right to ill-use them at their pleasure; and very often accompanied their commands with blows, whether the children were behaving well or ill. I have seen their flesh ragged and raw with licks.[25] – Lick – lick – they were never secure one moment from a blow, and their lives were passed in continual fear. My mistress was not contented with using the whip, but often pinched their cheeks and arms in the most cruel manner. My pity for these poor boys was soon transferred to myself; for I was licked, and flogged, and pinched by her pitiless fingers in the neck and arms, exactly as they were. To strip me naked – to hang me up by the wrists and lay my flesh open with the cow-skin, was an ordinary punishment for even a slight offence. My mistress often robbed me too of the hours that belong to sleep. She used to sit up very late, frequently even until morning; and I had then to stand at a bench and wash during the greater part of the night, or pick wool and cotton; and often I have dropped down overcome by sleep and fatigue, till roused from a state of stupor by the whip, and forced to start up to my tasks.

Poor Hetty, my fellow slave, was very kind to me, and I used to call her my Aunt; but she led a most miserable life, and her death was hastened (at least the slaves all believed and said so,) by the dreadful chastisement she received from my master during her pregnancy.[26] It happened as follows. One of the cows had dragged the rope away from the stake to which Hetty had fastened it, and got loose. My master flew into a terrible passion, and ordered the poor creature to be stripped quite naked, notwithstanding her pregnancy, and to be tied up to a tree in the yard. He then flogged her as hard as he could lick, both with the whip and cow-skin, till she was all over streaming with blood. He rested, and then beat her again and again. Her shrieks were terrible. The consequence was that poor Hetty was brought to bed before her time, and was delivered after severe labour of a dead child. She appeared to recover after her confinement, so far that she was repeatedly flogged by both master and mistress afterwards; but her former strength never returned to her. Ere long her body and limbs swelled to a great size; and she lay on a mat in the kitchen, till the water burst out of her body and she died. All the slaves said that death was a good thing for poor Hetty; but I cried very much for her death. The manner of it filled me with horror. I could not bear to think about it; yet it was always present to my mind for many a day.

After Hetty died all her labours fell upon me, in addition to my own. I had now to milk eleven cows every morning before sunrise, sitting among the damp weeds; to take care of the cattle as well as the children; and to do the work of the house. There was no end to my toils – no end to my blows. I lay down at night and rose up in the morning in fear and sorrow; and often wished that like poor Hetty I could escape from this cruel bondage and be at rest in the grave. But the hand of that God whom then I knew not, was stretched over me; and I was mercifully preserved for better things. It was then, however, my heavy lot to weep, weep, weep, and that for years; to pass from one misery to another, and from one cruel master to a worse. But I must go on with the thread of my story.

One day a heavy squall of wind and rain came on suddenly, and my mistress sent me round the corner of the house to empty a large earthen jar. The jar was already cracked with an old deep crack that divided it in the middle, and in turning it upside down to empty it, it parted in my hand. I could not help the accident, but I was dreadfully frightened, looking forward to a severe punishment. I ran crying to my mistress, 'O mistress, the jar has come in two.' 'You have broken it, have you?' she replied; 'come directly here to me.' I came trembling: she stripped and flogged me long and severely with the cow-skin; as long as she had strength to use the lash, for she did not give over till she was quite tired. – When my master came home at night, she told him of my fault; and oh, frightful! how he fell a swearing. After abusing me with every ill name he could think of, (too, too bad to speak in England,) and giving me several heavy blows with his hand, he said, 'I shall come home to-morrow morning at twelve, on purpose to give you a round hundred.' He kept his word – Oh sad for me! I cannot easily forget it. He tied me up upon a ladder, and gave me a hundred lashes with his own hand, and master Benjy stood by to count them for him. When he had licked me for some time he sat down to take breath; then after resting, he beat me again and again, until he was quite wearied, and so hot (for the weather was very sultry), that he sank back in his chair, almost like to faint. While my mistress went to bring him drink, there was a dreadful earthquake. Part of the roof fell down, and every thing in the house went – clatter, clatter, clatter. Oh I thought the end of all things near at hand; and I was so sore with the flogging, that I scarcely cared whether I lived or died. The earth was groaning and shaking; every thing tumbling about; and my mistress and the slaves were shrieking and crying out, 'The earthquake! the earthquake!' It was an awful day for us all.

During the confusion I crawled away on my hands and knees, and laid myself down under the steps of the piazza, in front of the house. I was in a dreadful state – my body all blood and bruises, and I could not help moaning piteously. The other slaves, when they saw me, shook their heads and said, 'Poor child! poor child!' – I lay there till the morning, careless of what might happen, for life was very weak in me, and I wished more than ever to die. But when we are very young, death always seems a great way off, and it would not come that night to me. The next morning I was forced by my master to rise and go about my usual work, though my body and limbs were so stiff and sore, that I could not move without the greatest pain. – Nevertheless, even after all this severe punishment, I never heard the last of that jar; my mistress was always throwing it in my face.

Some little time after this, one of the cows got loose from the stake, and eat one of the sweet-potatoe slips.[27] I was milking when my master found it out. He came to me, and without any more ado, stooped down, and taking off his heavy boot, he struck me such a severe blow in the small of my back, that I shrieked with agony, and thought I was killed; and I feel a weakness in that part to this day. The cow was frightened at his violence, and kicked down the pail and spilt the milk all about. My master knew that this accident was his own fault, but he was so enraged that he seemed glad of an excuse to go on with his ill usage. I cannot remember how many licks he gave me then, but he beat me till I was unable to stand, and till he himself was weary.

After this I ran away and went to my mother, who was living with Mr Richard Darrel. My poor mother was both grieved and glad to see me; grieved because I had been so ill used, and glad because she had not seen me for a long, long while. She dared not receive me into the house, but she hid me up in a hole in the rocks near, and brought me food at night, after every body was asleep. My father, who lived at Crow-Lane, over the salt-water channel,[28] last heard of my being hid up in the cavern, and he came and took me back to my master. Oh I was loth, loth to go back; but as there was no remedy, I was obliged to submit.

When we got home, my poor father said to Capt. I—, 'Sir, I am sorry that my child should be forced to run away from her owner; but the treatment she has received is enough to break her heart. The sight of her wounds has nearly broke mine. – I entreat you, for the love of God, to forgive her for running away, and that you will be a kind master to her in future.' Capt. I— said I was used as well as I deserved, and that I ought to be punished for running away. I then took courage and said that I could stand the floggings no longer; that I was weary of my life, and therefore I had run away to my mother; but mothers could only weep and mourn over their children, they could not save them from cruel masters – from the whip, the rope, and the cow-skin. He told me to hold my tongue and go about my work, or he would find a way to settle me. He did not, however, flog me that day.

For five years after this I remained in his house, and almost daily received the same harsh treatment. At length he put me on board a sloop,[29] and to my great joy sent me away to Turk's Island.[30] I was not permitted to see my mother or father, or poor sisters and brothers, to say good bye, though going away to a strange land, and might never see them again. Oh the Buckra people[31] who keep slaves think that black people are like cattle, without natural affection. But my heart tells me it is far otherwise.

We were nearly four weeks on the voyage, which was unusually long. Sometimes we had a light breeze, sometimes a great calm, and the ship made no way; so that our provisions and water ran very low, and we were put upon short allowance. I should almost have been starved had it not been for the kindness of a black man called Anthony, and his wife, who had brought their own victuals, and shared them with me.

When we went ashore at the Grand Quay,[32] the captain sent me to the house of my new master, Mr D—, to whom Captain I— had sold me. Grand Quay is a small town upon a sandbank; the houses low and built of wood. Such was my new master's. The first person I saw, on my arrival, was Mr D—, a stout sulky looking man, who carried me through the hall to show me to his wife and children. Next day I was put up by the vendue master to know how much I was worth, and I was valued at one hundred pounds currency.

My new master was one of the owners or holders of the salt ponds,[33] and he received a certain sum for every slave that worked upon his premises, whether they were young or old. This sum was allowed him out of the profits arising from the salt works. I was immediately sent to work in the salt water with the rest of the slaves. This work was perfectly new to me. I was given a half barrel and a shovel, and had to stand up to my knees in the water, from four o'clock in the morning till nine, when we were given some Indian corn[34] boiled in water, which we were obliged to swallow as fast as we could for fear the rain should come on and melt the salt. We were then called again to our tasks, and worked through the heat of the day; the sun flaming upon our heads like fire, and raising salt blisters in those parts which were not completely covered. Our feet and legs, from standing in the salt water for so many hours, soon became full of dreadful boils, which eat down in some cases to the very bone, afflicting the sufferers with great torment. We came home at twelve; ate our corn soup, called *blawly*, as fast as we could, and went back to our employment till dark at night. We then shovelled up the salt in large heaps, and went down to the sea, where we washed the pickle from our limbs, and cleaned the barrows and shovels from the salt. When we returned to the house, our master gave us each our allowance of raw Indian corn, which we pounded in a mortar and boiled in water for our suppers.

We slept in a long shed, divided into narrow slips, like the stalls used for cattle. Boards fixed upon stakes driven into the ground, without mat or covering, were our only beds. On Sundays, after we had washed the salt bags, and done other work required of us, we went into the bush and cut the long soft grass, of which we made trusses[35] for our legs and feet to rest upon, for they were so full of the salt boils that we could get no rest lying upon the bare boards.

Though we worked from morning till night, there was no satisfying Mr D—. I hoped, when I left Capt. I—, that I should have been better off, but I found it was but going from one butcher to another. There was this difference between them: my former master used to beat me while raging and foaming with passion; Mr D— was usually quite calm. He would stand by and give orders for a slave to be cruelly whipped, and assist in the punishment, without moving a muscle of his face; walking about and taking snuff with the greatest composure. Nothing could touch his hard heart – neither sighs, nor tears, nor prayers, nor streaming blood; he was deaf to our cries, and careless of our sufferings. – Mr D— has often stripped me naked, hung me up by the wrists, and beat me with the cow-skin, with his own hand, till my body was raw with gashes. Yet there was nothing very remarkable in this; for it might serve as a sample of the common usage of the slaves on that horrible island.

Owing to the boils in my feet, I was unable to wheel the barrow fast through the sand, which got into the sores, and made me stumble at every step; and my master, having no pity for my sufferings from this cause, rendered them far more intolerable, by chastising me for not being able to move so fast as he wished me. Another of our employments was to row a little way off from the shore in a boat, and dive for large stones to build a wall round our master's house. This was very hard work; and the great waves breaking over us continually, made us often so giddy that we lost our footing, and were in danger of being drowned.

Ah, poor me! – my tasks were never ended. Sick or well, it was work – work – work! – After the diving season[36] was over, we were sent to the South Creek,[37] with large bills, to cut up mangoes to burn lime with.[38] Whilst one party of slaves were thus employed, another were sent to the other side of the island to break up coral out of the sea.

When we were ill, let our complaint be what it might, the only medicine given to us was a great bowl of hot salt water, with salt mixed with it, which made us very sick. If we could not keep up with the rest of the gang of slaves, we were put in the stocks, and severely flogged the next morning. Yet, not the less, our master expected, after we had thus been kept from our rest, and our limbs rendered stiff and sore with ill usage, that we should still go through the ordinary tasks of the day all the same. – Sometimes we had to work all night, measuring salt to load a vessel; or turning a machine to draw water out of the sea for the salt-making. Then we had no sleep – no rest – but were forced to work as fast as we could, and go on again all next day the same as usual. Work – work – work – Oh that Turk's Island was a horrible place! The people in England, I am sure, have never found out what is carried on there. Cruel, horrible place!

Mr D— had a slave called old Daniel, whom he used to treat in the most cruel manner. Poor Daniel was lame in the hip, and could not keep up with the rest of the slaves; and our master would order him to be stripped and laid down on the ground, and have him beaten with a rod of rough briar till his skin was quite red and raw. He would then call for a bucket of salt, and fling upon the raw flesh till the man writhed on the ground like a worm, and screamed aloud with agony. This poor man's wounds were never healed, and I have often seen them full of maggots, which increased his torments to an intolerable degree. He was an object of pity and terror to the whole gang of slaves, and in his wretched case we saw, each of us, our own lot, if we should live to be as old.

Oh the horrors of slavery! – How the thought of it pains my heart! But the truth ought to be told of it; and what my eyes have seen I think it is my duty to relate; for few people in England know what slavery is. I have been a slave – I have felt what a slave feels, and I know what a slave knows; and I would have all the good people in England to know it too, that they may break our chains, and set us free.

Mr D— had another slave called Ben. He being very hungry, stole a little rice one night after he came in from work, and cooked it for his supper. But his master soon discovered the theft; locked him up all night; and kept him without food till one o'clock the next day. He then hung Ben up by his hands, and beat him from time to time till the slaves came in at night. We found the poor creature hung up when we came home; with a pool of blood beneath him, and our master still licking him. But this was not the worst. My master's son was in the habit of stealing the rice and rum. Ben had seen him do this, and thought he might do the same, and when master found out that Ben had stolen the rice and swore to punish him, he tried to excuse himself by saying that Master Dickey did the same thing every night. The lad denied it to his father, and was so angry with Ben for informing against him, that out of revenge he ran and got a bayonet, and whilst the poor wretch was suspended by his hands and writhing under his wounds, he run it quite through his foot. I was not by when he did it, but I saw the wound when I came home, and heard Ben tell the manner in which it was done.

I must say something more about this cruel son of a cruel father. – He had no heart – no fear of God; he had been brought up by a bad father in a bad path, and he delighted to follow in the same steps. There was a little old woman among the slaves called Sarah, who was nearly past work; and, Master Dickey being the overseer of the slaves[39] just then, this poor creature, who was subject to several bodily infirmities, and was not quite right in her head, did not wheel the barrow fast enough to please him. He threw her down on the ground, and after beating her severely, he took her up in his arms and flung her among the prickly-pear bushes,[40] which are all covered over with sharp venomous prickles. By this her naked flesh was so grievously wounded, that her body swelled and festered all over, and she died a few days after. In telling my own sorrows, I cannot pass by those of my fellow-slaves – for when I think of my own griefs, I remember theirs.

I think it was about ten years I had worked in the salt ponds at Turk's Island, when my master left off business, and retired to a house he had in Bermuda, leaving his son to succeed him in the island. He took me with him to wait upon his daughters; and I was joyful, for I was sick, sick of Turk's Island, and my heart yearned to see my native place again, my mother, and my kindred.

I had seen my poor mother during the time I was a slave in Turk's Island. One Sunday morning I was on the beach with some of the slaves, and we saw a sloop come in loaded with slaves to work in the salt water.[41] We got a boat and went aboard. When I came upon the deck I asked the black people, 'Is there any one here for me?' 'Yes,' they said, 'your mother.' I thought they said this in jest – I could scarcely believe them for joy; but when I saw my poor mammy my joy was turned to sorrow, for she had gone from her senses. 'Mammy,' I said, 'is this you?' She did not know me. 'Mammy,' I said, 'what's the matter?' She began to talk foolishly, and said that she had been under the vessel's bottom. They had been overtaken by a violent storm at sea. My poor mother had never been on the sea before, and she was so ill, that she lost her senses, and it was long before she came quite to herself again. She had a sweet child with her – a little sister I had never seen, about four years of age, called Rebecca. I took her on shore with me, for I felt I should love her directly; and I kept her with me a week. Poor little thing! her's has been a sad life, and continues so to this day. My mother worked for some years on the island, but was taken back to Bermuda some time before my master carried me again thither.*

After I left Turk's Island, I was told by some negroes that came over from it, that the poor slaves had built up a place with boughs and leaves, where they might meet for prayers, but the white people pulled it down twice, and would not allow them even a shed for prayers. A flood came down soon after and washed away many houses, filled the place with sand, and overflowed the ponds: and I do think that this was for their wickedness; for the Buckra men† there were very wicked. I saw and heard much that was very very bad at that place.

I was several years the slave of Mr D— after I returned to my native place. Here I worked in the grounds. My work was planting and

* Of the subsequent lot of her relatives she can tell but little. She says, her father died while she and her mother were at Turk's Island; and that he had been long dead and buried before any of his children in Bermuda knew it, they being slaves on other estates. Her mother died after Mary went to Antigua. Of the fate of the rest of her kindred, seven brothers and three sisters, she knows nothing further than this – that the eldest sister, who had several children to her master, was taken by him to Trinidad; and that the youngest, Rebecca, is still alive, and in slavery in Bermuda. Mary herself is now about forty-three years of age. – Ed.

† Negro term for white people.

hoeing sweet-potatoes, Indian corn, plaintains,[42] bananas, cabbages, pumpkins, onions, &c. I did all the household work, and attended upon a horse and cow besides, – going also upon all errands. I had to curry the horse – to clean and feed him – and sometimes to ride him a little. I had more than enough to do – but still it was not so very bad as Turk's Island.

My old master often got drunk, and then he would get in a fury with his daughter, and beat her till she was not fit to be seen. I remember on one occasion, I had gone to fetch water, and when I was coming up the hill I heard a great screaming; I ran as fast as I could to the house, put down the water, and went into the chamber, where I found my master beating Miss D— dreadfully. I strove with all my strength to get her away from him; for she was all black and blue with bruises. He had beat her with his fist, and almost killed her. The people gave me credit for getting her away. He turned round and began to lick me. Then I said, 'Sir, this is not Turk's Island.' I can't repeat his answer, the words were too wicked – too bad to say. He wanted to treat me the same in Bermuda as he had done in Turk's Island.

He had an ugly fashion of stripping himself quite naked, and ordering me then to wash him in a tub of water. This was worse to me than all the licks. Sometimes when he called me to wash him I could not come, my eyes were so full of shame. He would then come to beat me. One time I had plates and knives in my hand, and I dropped both plates and knives, and some of the plates were broken. He struck me so severely for this, that at last I defended myself, for I thought it was high time to do so. I then told him I would not live longer with him, for he was a very indecent man – very spiteful, and too indecent; with no shame for his servants, no shame for his own flesh. So I went away to a neighbouring house and sat down and cried till the next morning, when I went home again, not knowing what else to do.

After that I was hired to work at Cedar Hills[43] and every Saturday night I paid the money to my master. I had plenty of work to do there – plenty of washing; but yet I made myself pretty comfortable. I earned two dollars and a quarter a week, which is twenty pence a day.

During the time I worked there, I heard that Mr John Wood was going to Antigua.[44] I felt a great wish to go there, and I went to Mr D—, and asked him to let me go in Mr Wood's service. Mr Wood did not then want to purchase me; it was my own fault that I came under him, I was so anxious to go. It was ordained to be, I suppose; God led me there. The truth is, I did not wish to be any longer the slave of my indecent master.

Mr Wood took me with him to Antigua, to the town of St John's,[45] where he lived. This was about fifteen years ago.[46] He did not then know whether I was to be sold; but Mrs Wood found that I could work, and she wanted to buy me. Her husband then wrote to my master to inquire whether I was to be sold? Mr D— wrote in reply, 'that I should not be sold to any one that would treat me ill.' It was strange he should say this, when he had treated me so ill himself. So I was purchased by Mr Wood for 300 dollars, (or £100 Bermuda currency.)*

My work there was to attend the chambers and nurse the child, and to go down to the pond and wash clothes. But I soon fell ill of the rheumatism, and grew so very lame that I was forced to walk with a stick. I got the Saint Anthony's fire,[47] also, in my left leg, and became quite a cripple. No one cared much to come near me, and I was ill a long long time; for several months I could not lift the limb. I had to lie in a little old out-house, that was swarming with bugs and other vermin, which tormented me greatly; but I had no other place to lie in. I got the rheumatism by catching cold at the pond side, from washing in the fresh water; in the salt water I never got cold. The person who lived in next yard, (a Mrs Greene,) could not bear to hear my cries and groans. She was kind, and used to send an old slave woman to help me, who sometimes brought me a little soup. When the doctor found I was so ill, he said I must be put into a bath of hot water. The old slave got the bark of some bush that was good for the pains, which she boiled in the hot water, and every night she came and put me into the bath, and did what she could for me: I don't know what I should have done, or what would have become of me,

---

* About £67. 10s. sterling.

had it not been for her. – My mistress, it is true, did send me a little food; but no one from our family came near me but the cook, who used to shove my food in at the door, and say, 'Molly, Molly, there's your dinner.' My mistress did not care to take any trouble about me; and if the Lord had not put it into the hearts of the neighbours to be kind to me, I must, I really think, have lain and died.

It was a long time before I got well enough to work in the house. Mrs Wood, in the meanwhile, hired a mulatto woman to nurse the child; but she was such a fine lady she wanted to be mistress over me. I thought it very hard for a coloured woman to have rule over me because I was a slave and she was free. Her name was Martha Wilcox; she was a saucy woman, very saucy; and she went and complained of me, without cause, to my mistress, and made her angry with me. Mrs Wood told me that if I did not mind what I was about, she would get my master to strip me and give me fifty lashes: 'You have been used to the whip,' she said, 'and you shall have it here.' This was the first time she threatened to have me flogged; and she gave me the threatening so strong of what she would have done to me, that I thought I should have fallen down at her feet, I was so vexed and hurt by her words. The mulatto woman was rejoiced to have power to keep me down. She was constantly making mischief; there was no living for the slaves – no peace after she came.

I was also sent by Mrs Wood to be put in the Cage[48] one night, and was next morning flogged, by the magistrate's order, at her desire; and this all for a quarrel I had about a pig with another slave woman.[49] I was flogged on my naked back on this occasion: although I was in no fault after all; for old Justice Dyett, when we came before him, said that I was in the right, and ordered the pig to be given to me. This was about two or three years after I came to Antigua.

When we moved from the middle of the town to the Point,[50] I used to be in the house and do all the work and mind the children, though still very ill with the rheumatism. Every week I had to wash two large bundles of clothes, as much as a boy could help me to lift; but I could give no satisfaction. My mistress was always abusing and fretting after me. It is not possible to tell all her ill language. – One day she followed me foot after foot scolding and rating me. I bore in silence a great deal of ill words: at last my heart was quite full, and I told her that she ought not to use me so; – that when I was ill I might have lain and died for what she cared; and no one would then come near me to nurse me, because they were afraid of my mistress. This was a great affront. She called her husband and told him what I had said. He flew into a passion: but did not beat me then; he only abused and swore at me; and then gave me a note and bade me go and look for an owner. Not that he meant to sell me; but he did this to please his wife and to frighten me. I went to Adam White, a cooper,[51] a free black, who had money, and asked him to buy me. He went directly to Mr Wood, but was informed that I was not to be sold. The next day my master whipped me.

Another time (about five years ago) my mistress got vexed with me, because I fell sick and I could not keep on with my work. She complained to her husband, and he sent me off again to look for an owner. I went to a Mr Burchell, showed him the note, and asked him to buy me for my own benefit; for I had saved about 100 dollars, and hoped, with a little help, to purchase my freedom. He accordingly went to my master: – 'Mr Wood,' he said, 'Molly has brought me a note that she wants an owner. If you intend to sell her, I may as well buy her as another.' My master put him off and said that he did not mean to sell me. I was very sorry at this, for I had no comfort with Mrs Wood, and I wished greatly to get my freedom.

The way in which I made my money was this. – When my master and mistress went from home, as they sometimes did, and left me to take care of the house and premises, I had a good deal of time to myself, and made the most of it. I took in washing, and sold coffee and yams and other provisions to the captains of ships. I did not sit still idling during the absence of my owners; for I wanted, by all honest means, to earn money to buy my freedom. Sometimes I bought a hog cheap on board ship, and sold it for double the money on shore; and I also earned a good deal by selling coffee. By this means I by degrees acquired a little cash. A gentleman also lent me some to help to buy my freedom – but when I could not get free he got it back again. His name was Captain Abbot.[52]

My master and mistress went on one occasion into the country, to

Date Hill, for change of air, and carried me with them to take charge of the children, and to do the work of the house. While I was in the country, I saw how the field negroes are worked in Antigua. They are worked very hard and fed but scantily. They are called out to work before daybreak, and come home after dark; and then each has to heave his bundle of grass for the cattle in the pen. Then, on Sunday morning, each slave has to go out and gather a large bundle of grass; and, when they bring it home, they have all to sit at the manager's door and wait till he come out: often they have to wait there till past eleven o'clock, without any breakfast. After that, those that have yams or potatoes, or fire-wood to sell, hasten to market to buy a dog's worth* of salt fish,[53] or pork, which is a great treat for them. Some of them buy a little pickle out of the shad barrels,[54] which they call sauce, to season their yams and Indian corn. It is very wrong, I know, to work on Sunday or go to market; but will not God call the Buckra men to answer for this on the great day of judgment – since they will give the slaves no other day?

While we were at Date Hill Christmas came; and the slave woman who had the care of the place (which then belonged to Mr Roberts the marshal),[55] asked me to go with her to her husband's house, to a Methodist meeting[56] for prayer, at a plantation called Winthorps. I went; and they were the first prayers I ever understood. One woman prayed; and then they all sung a hymn; then there was another prayer and another hymn; and then they all spoke by turns of their own griefs as sinners. The husband of the woman I went with was a black driver.[57] His name was Henry. He confessed that he had treated the slaves very cruelly; but said that he was compelled to obey the orders of his master. He prayed them all to forgive him, and he prayed that God would forgive him. He said it was a horrid thing for a ranger† to have sometimes to beat his own wife or sister; but he must do so if ordered by his master.

I felt sorry for my sins also. I cried the whole night, but I was too

---

* A dog is the 72nd part of a dollar.

† The head negro of an estate – a person who has the chief superintendence under the manager.

much ashamed to speak. I prayed God to forgive me. This meeting had a great impression on my mind, and led my spirit to the Moravian church;[58] so that when I got back to town, I went and prayed to have my name put down in the Missionaries' book; and I followed the church earnestly every opportunity.[59] I did not then tell my mistress about it; for I knew that she would not give me leave to go. But I felt I *must* go. Whenever I carried the children their lunch at school, I ran round and went to hear the teachers.

The Moravian ladies (Mrs Richter, Mrs Olufsen, and Mrs Sauter) taught me to read in the class; and I got on very fast. In this class there were all sorts of people, old and young, grey headed folks and children; but most of them were free people. After we had done spelling, we tried to read in the Bible. After the reading was over, the missionary gave out a hymn for us to sing. I dearly loved to go to the church, it was so solemn. I never knew rightly that I had much sin till I went there. When I found out that I was a great sinner, I was very sorely grieved, and very much frightened. I used to pray God to pardon my sins for Christ's sake, and forgive me for every thing I had done amiss; and when I went home to my work, I always thought about what I had heard from the missionaries, and wished to be good that I might go to heaven. After a while I was admitted a candidate for the holy Communion. – I had been baptized long before this, in the year 1817, by the Rev. Mr Curtin, of the English Church, after I had been taught to repeat the Creed and the Lord's Prayer. I wished at that time to attend a Sunday School taught by Mr Curtin, but he would not receive me without a written note from my master, granting his permission. I did not ask my owner's permission, from the belief that it would be refused; so that I got no farther instruction at that time from the English Church.*

---

* She possesses a copy of Mrs Trimmer's 'Charity School Spelling Book,' presented to her by the Rev. Mr Curtin, and dated August 30, 1817. In this book her name is written 'Mary, Princess of Wales' – an appellation which, she says, was given her by her owners. It is a common practice with the colonists to give ridiculous names of this description to their slaves; being, in fact, one of the numberless modes of expressing the habitual contempt with which they regard the negro race. – In printing this narrative we have retained Mary's paternal name of Prince. – *Ed.*

Some time after I began to attend the Moravian Church, I met with Daniel James, afterwards my dear husband. He was a carpenter and cooper to his trade; an honest, hard-working, decent black man, and a widower. He had purchased his freedom of his mistress, old Mrs Baker, with money he had earned whilst a slave. When he asked me to marry him, I took time to consider the matter over with myself, and would not say yes till he went to church with me and joined the Moravians. He was very industrious after he bought his freedom; and he had hired a comfortable house, and had convenient things about him. We were joined in marriage, about Christmas 1826, in the Moravian Chapel at Spring Gardens, by the Rev. Mr Olufsen.[60] We could not be married in the English Church. English marriage[61] is not allowed to slaves; and no free man can marry a slave woman.

When Mr Wood heard of my marriage, he flew into a great rage, and sent for Daniel, who was helping to build a house for his old mistress. Mr Wood asked him who gave him a right to marry a slave of his? My husband said, 'Sir, I am a free man, and thought I had a right to choose a wife; but if I had known Molly was not allowed to have a husband, I should not have asked her to marry me.' Mrs Wood was more vexed about my marriage than her husband. She could not forgive me for getting married, but stirred up Mr Wood to flog me dreadfully with the horsewhip. I thought it very hard to be whipped at my time of life for getting a husband – I told her so. She said that she would not have nigger men about the yards of premises, or allow a nigger man's clothes to be washed in the same tub where hers were washed. She was fearful, I think, that I should lose her time, in order to wash and do things for my husband; but I had then no time to wash for myself; I was obliged to put out my own clothes, though I was always at the wash-tub.

I had not much happiness in my marriage, owing to my being a slave. It made my husband sad to see me so ill-treated. Mrs Wood was always abusing me about him. She did not lick me herself, but she got her husband to do it for her, whilst she fretted the flesh off my bones. Yet for all this she would not sell me. She sold five slaves whilst I was with her; but though she was always finding fault with me, she would not part with me. However, Mr Wood afterwards allowed Daniel to have a place to live in our yard, which we were very thankful for.

After this, I fell ill again with the rheumatism, and was sick a long time; but whether sick or well, I had my work to do. About this time I asked my master and mistress to let me buy my own freedom. With the help of Mr Burchell, I could have found the means to pay Mr Wood; for it was agreed that I should afterwards serve Mr Burchell a while, for the cash he was to advance for me. I was earnest in the request to my owners; but their hearts were hard – too hard to consent. Mrs Wood was very angry – she grew quite outrageous – she called me a black devil, and asked me who had put freedom into my head. 'To be free is very sweet,' I said: but she took good care to keep me a slave. I saw her change colour, and I left the room.

About this time my master and mistress were going to England to put their son to school, and bring their daughters home; and they took me with them to take care of the child. I was willing to come to England: I thought that by going there I should probably get cured of my rheumatism, and should return with my master and mistress, quite well, to my husband. My husband was willing for me to come away, for he had heard that my master would free me, – and I also hoped this might prove true; but it was all a false report.

The steward of the ship was very kind to me. He and my husband were in the same class in the Moravian Church. I was thankful that he was so friendly, for my mistress was not kind to me on the passage; and she told me, when she was angry, that she did not intend to treat me any better in England than in the West Indies – that I need not expect it. And she was as good as her word.

When we drew near to England, the rheumatism seized all my limbs worse than ever, and my body was dreadfully swelled. When we landed at the Tower,[62] I shewed my flesh to my mistress, but she took no great notice of it. We were obliged to stop at the tavern till my master got a house; and a day or two after, my mistress sent me down into the wash-house to learn to wash in the English way. In the West Indies we wash with cold water – in England with hot. I told my mistress I was afraid that putting my hands first into the hot water and then into the cold, would increase the pain in my limbs.

The doctor had told my mistress long before I came from the West Indies, that I was a sickly body and the washing did not agree with me. But Mrs Wood would not release me from the tub, so I was forced to do as I could. I grew worse, and could not stand to wash. I was then forced to sit down with the tub before me, and often through pain and weakness was reduced to kneel or to sit down on the floor, to finish my task. When I complained to my mistress of this, she only got into a passion as usual, and said washing in hot water could not hurt any one; – that I was lazy and insolent, and wanted to be free of my work; but that she would make me do it. I thought her very hard on me, and my heart rose up within me. However I kept still at that time, and went down again to wash the child's things; but the English washerwomen who were at work there, when they saw that I was so ill, had pity upon me and washed them for me.

After that, when we came up to live in Leigh Street,[63] Mrs Wood sorted out five bags of clothes which we had used at sea, and also such as had been worn since we came on shore, for me and the cook to wash. Elizabeth the cook told her, that she did not think that I was able to stand to the tub, and that she had better hire a woman. I also said myself, that I had come over to nurse the child, and that I was sorry I had come from Antigua, since mistress would work me so hard, without compassion for my rheumatism. Mr and Mrs Wood, when they heard this, rose up in a passion against me. They opened the door and bade me get out. But I was a stranger, and did not know one door in the street from another, and was unwilling to go away. They made a dreadful uproar, and from that day they constantly kept cursing and abusing me. I was obliged to wash, though I was very ill. Mrs Wood, indeed once hired a washerwoman, but she was not well treated, and would come no more.

My master quarrelled with me another time, about one of our great washings, his wife having stirred him up to do so. He said he would compel me to do the whole of the washing given out to me, or if I again refused, he would take a short course with me: he would either send me down to the brig[64] in the river, to carry me back to Antigua, or he would turn me at once out of doors, and let me provide for myself. I said I would willingly go back, if he would let me purchase my own freedom. But this enraged him more than all the rest: he cursed and swore at me dreadfully, and said he would never sell my freedom – if I wished to be free, I was free in England,[65] and I might go and try what freedom would do for me, and be d—d. My heart was very sore with this treatment, but I had to go on. I continued to do my work, and did all I could to give satisfaction, but all would not do.

Shortly after, the cook left them, and then matters went on ten times worse. I always washed the child's clothes without being commanded to do it, and any thing else that was wanted in the family; though still I was very sick – very sick indeed. When the great washing came round, which was every two months, my mistress got together again a great many heavy things, such as bed-ticks,[66] bed-coverlets, &c. for me to wash. I told her I was too ill to wash such heavy things that day. She said, she supposed I thought myself a free woman, but I was not; and if I did not do it directly I should be instantly turned out of doors. I stood a long time before I could answer, for I did not know well what to do. I knew that I was free in England, but I did not know where to go, or how to get my living; and therefore, I did not like to leave the house. But Mr Wood said he would send for a constable to thrust me out; and at last I took course and resolved that I would not be longer thus treated, but would go and trust to Providence. This was the fourth time they had threatened to turn me out, and, go where I might, I was determined now to take them at their word; though I thought it very hard, after I had lived with them for thirteen years, and worked for them like a horse, to be driven out in this way, like a beggar. My only fault was being sick, and therefore unable to please my mistress, who thought she never could get work enough out of her slaves; and I told them so: but they only abused me and drove me out. This took place from two to three months, I think, after we came to England.

When I came away, I went to the man (one Mash) who used to black the shoes[67] of the family, and asked his wife to get somebody to go with me to Hatton Garden[68] to the Moravian Missionaries: these were the only persons I knew in England. The woman sent a young girl with me to the mission house, and I saw there a gentleman called Mr Moore. I told him my whole story, and how my owners had treated me, and asked him to take in my trunk with what few clothes I had. The missionaries were very kind to me – they were sorry for my destitute situation, and gave me leave to bring my things to be placed under their care. They were very good people, and they told me to come to the church.

When I went back to Mr Wood's to get my trunk, I saw a lady, Mrs Pell, who was on a visit to my mistress. When Mr and Mrs Wood heard me come in, they set this lady to stop me, finding that they had gone too far with me. Mrs Pell came out to me, and said, 'Are you really going to leave, Molly? Don't leave, but come into the country with me.' I believe she said this because she thought Mrs Wood would easily get me back again. I replied to her, 'Ma'am, this is the fourth time my master and mistress have driven me out, or threatened to drive me – and I will give them no more occasion to bid me go. I was not willing to leave them, for I am a stranger in this country, but now I must go – I can stay no longer to be so used.' Mrs Pell then went up stairs to my mistress, and told that I would go, and that she could not stop me. Mrs Wood was very much hurt and frightened when she found I was determined to go out that day. She said, 'If she goes the people will rob her, and then turn her adrift.' She did not say this to me, but she spoke it loud enough for me to hear; that it might induce me not to go, I suppose. Mr Wood also asked me where I was going to. I told him where I had been, and that I should never have gone away had I not been driven out by my owners. He had given me a written paper some time before, which said that I had come with them to England by my own desire; and that was true. It said also that I left them of my own free will, because I was a free woman in England; and that I was idle and would not do my work – which was not true. I gave this paper afterwards to a gentleman who inquired into my case.*[69]

I went into the kitchen and got my clothes out. The nurse and the servant girl were there, and I said to the man who was going to take out my trunk, 'Stop, before you take up this trunk, and hear what I

* See page 24 [p. 39 of this edition].

have to say before these people. I am going out of this house, as I was ordered; but I have done no wrong at all to my owners, neither here nor in the West Indies. I always worked very hard to please them, both by night and day; but there was no giving satisfaction, for my mistress could never be satisfied with reasonable service. I told my mistress I was sick, and yet she has ordered me out of doors. This is the fourth time; and now I am going out.'

And so I came out, and went and carried my trunk to the Moravians. I then returned back to Mash the shoe-black's house, and begged his wife to take me in. I had a little West Indian money in my trunk; and they got it changed for me. This helped to support me for a little while. The man's wife was very kind to me. I was very sick, and she boiled nourishing things up for me. She also sent for a doctor to see me, and he sent me medicine, which did me good, though I was ill for a long time with the rheumatic pains. I lived a good many months with these poor people, and they nursed me, and did all that lay in their power to serve me. The man was well acquainted with my situation, as he used to go to and fro to Mr Wood's house to clean shoes and knives; and he and his wife were sorry for me.

About this time, a woman of the name of Hill told me of the Anti-Slavery Society, and went with me to their office, to inquire if they could do any thing to get me my freedom, and send me back to the West Indies. The gentlemen of the Society took me to a lawyer, who examined very strictly into my case; but told me that the laws of England could do nothing to make me free in Antigua.* However they did all they could for me: they gave me a little money from time to time to keep me from want; and some of them went to Mr Wood to try to persuade him to let me return a free woman to my husband; but though they offered him, as I have heard, a large sum for my freedom, he was sulky and obstinate, and would not consent to let me go free.

This was the first winter I spent in England, and I suffered much

---

* She came first to the Anti-Slavery Office in Aldermanbury,[d] about the latter end of November 1828; and her case was referred to Mr George Stephen[e] to be investigated. More of this hereafter. – ED.

from the severe cold, and from the rheumatic pains, which still at times torment me. However, Providence was very good to me, and I got many friends – especially some Quaker ladies, who hearing of my case, came and sought me out, and gave me good warm clothing and money. Thus I had great cause to bless God in my affliction.

When I got better I was anxious to get some work to do, as I was unwilling to eat the bread of idleness.[70] Mrs Mash, who was a laundress, recommended me to a lady for a charwoman.[71] She paid me very handsomely for what work I did, and I divided the money with Mrs Mash; for though very poor, they gave me food when my own money was done, and never suffered me to want.

In the spring, I got into service with a lady, who saw me at the house where I sometimes worked as a charwoman. This lady's name was Mrs Forsyth. She had been in the West Indies, and was accustomed to Blacks, and liked them. I was with her six months, and went with her to Margate.[72] She treated me well, and gave me a good character[73] when she left London.*

After Mrs Forsyth went away, I was again out of place, and went to lodgings, for which I paid two shillings a week, and found coals and candle.[74] After eleven weeks, the money I had saved in service was all gone, and I was forced to go back to the Anti-Slavery office to ask a supply, till I could get another situation. I did not like to go back – I did not like to be idle. I would rather work for my living than get it for nothing. They were very good to give me a supply, but I felt shame at being obliged to apply for relief whilst I had strength to work.

At last I went into the service of Mr and Mrs Pringle, where I have been ever since, and am as comfortable as I can be while separated from my dear husband, and away from my own country and all old friends and connections. My dear mistress teaches me daily to read the word of God, and takes great pains to make me understand it. I enjoy the great privilege of being enabled to attend church three times on the Sunday; and I have met with many kind friends since I have been here, both clergymen and others. The Rev. Mr Young, who lives

---

* She refers to a written certificate which will be inserted afterwards.

in the next house, has shown me much kindness, and taken much pains to instruct me, particularly while my master and mistress were absent in Scotland.[75] Nor must I forget, among my friends, the Rev. Mr Mortimer, the good clergyman of the parish, under whose ministry I have now sat for upwards of twelve months. I trust in God I have profited by what I have heard from him. He never keeps back the truth, and I think he has been the means of opening my eyes and ears much better to understand the word of God. Mr Mortimer tells me that he cannot open the eyes of my heart, but that I must pray to God to change my heart, and make me to know the truth, and the truth will make me free.

I still live in the hope that God will find a way to give me my liberty, and give me back to my husband. I endeavour to keep down my fretting, and to leave all to Him, for he knows what is good for me better than I know myself. Yet, I must confess, I find it a hard and heavy task to do so.

I am often much vexed, and I feel great sorrow when I hear some people in this country say, that the slaves do not need better usage, and do not want to be free.* They believe the foreign people,† who deceive them, and say slaves are happy. I say, Not so. How can slaves be happy when they have the halter round their neck and the whip upon their back? and are disgraced and thought no more of than beasts? – and are separated from their mothers, and husbands, and children, and sisters, just as cattle are sold and separated? Is it happiness for a driver in the field to take down his wife or sister or child, and strip them, and whip them in such a disgraceful manner? – women that have had children exposed in the open field to shame! There is no modesty or decency shown by the owner to his slaves; men, women, and children are exposed alike. Since I have been here I have often wondered how English people can go out into the West Indies and act in such a beastly manner. But when they go to the West Indies, they forget God and all feeling of shame, I think, since they can see

---

* The whole of this paragraph especially, is given as nearly as was possible in Mary's precise words.[f]

† She means West Indians.[g]

and do such things. They tie up slaves like hogs – moor* them up like cattle, and they lick them, so as hogs, or cattle, or horses never were flogged; – and yet they come home and say, and make some good people believe, that slaves don't want to get out of slavery. But they put a cloak about the truth. It is not so. All slaves want to be free – to be free is very sweet. I will say the truth to English people who may read this history that my good friend, Miss S—,[76] is now writing down for me. I have been a slave myself – I know what slaves feel – I can tell by myself what other slaves feel, and by what they have told me. The man that says slaves be quite happy in slavery – that they don't want to be free – that man is either ignorant or a lying person. I never heard a slave say so. I never heard a Buckra man say so, till I heard tell of it in England. Such people ought to be ashamed of themselves. They can't do without slaves, they say. What's the reason they can't do without slaves as well as in England? No slaves here – no whips – no stocks – no punishment, except for wicked people. They hire servants in England; and if they don't like them, they send them away: they can't lick them. Let them work ever so hard in England, they are far better off than slaves. If they get a bad master, they give warning and go hire to another. They have their liberty. That's just what *we* want. We don't mind hard work, if we had proper treatment, and proper wages like English servants, and proper time given in the week to keep us from breaking the Sabbath. But they won't give it: they will have work – work – work, night and day, sick or well, till we are quite done up;[77] and we must not speak up nor look amiss, however much we be abused. And then when we are quite done up, who cares for us, more than for a lame horse? This is slavery. I tell it, to let English people know the truth; and I hope they will never leave off to pray God, and call loud to the great King of England,[78] till all the poor blacks be given free, and slavery done up for evermore.

---

* A West Indian phrase: to fasten or tie up.

SUPPLEMENT

TO THE

HISTORY OF MARY PRINCE

BY THE EDITOR[1]

LEAVING Mary's narrative, for the present, without comment to the reader's reflections, I proceed to state some circumstances connected with her case which have fallen more particularly under my own notice, and which I consider it incumbent now to lay fully before the public.

About the latter end of November 1828, this poor woman found her way to the office of the Anti-Slavery Society in Aldermanbury, by the aid of a person who had become acquainted with her situation, and had advised her to apply there for advice and assistance. After some preliminary examination into the accuracy of the circumstances related by her, I went along with her to Mr George Stephen, solicitor and requested him to investigate and draw up a statement of her case, and have it submitted to counsel, in order to ascertain whether or not, under the circumstances, her freedom could be legally established on her return to Antigua. On this occasion, in Mr Stephen's presence and mine, she expressed, in very strong terms, her anxiety to return thither if she could go as a free person, and, at the same time, her extreme apprehensions of the fate that would probably await her if she returned as a slave. Her words were, 'I would rather go into my grave than go back a slave to Antigua, though I wish to go back to my husband very much – very much – very much! I am much afraid my owners would separate me from my husband, and use me very hard, or perhaps sell me for a field negro; – and slavery is too too bad. I would rather go into my grave!'

The paper which Mr Wood had given her before she left his house, was placed by her in Mr Stephen's hands. It was expressed in the following terms:–

39

'I have already told Molly, and now give it her in writing, in order that there may be no misunderstanding on her part, that as I brought her from Antigua at her own request and entreaty, and that she is consequently now free, she is of course at liberty to take her baggage and go where she pleases. And, in consequence of her late conduct, she must do one of two things – either quit the house, or return to Antigua by the earliest opportunity, as she does not evince a disposition to make herself useful. As she is a stranger in London, I do not wish to turn her out, or would do so, as two female servants are sufficient for my establishment. If after this she does remain, it will be only during her good behaviour: but on no consideration will I allow her wages or any other remuneration for her services.

'JOHN A. WOOD.'

'London, August 18, 1828.'

This paper, though not devoid of inconsistencies, which will be apparent to any attentive reader, is craftily expressed; and was well devised to serve the purpose which the writer had obviously in view, namely, to frustrate any appeal which the friendless black woman might make to the sympathy of strangers, and thus prevent her from obtaining an asylum, if she left his house, from any respectable family. As she had no one to refer to for a character in this country except himself, he doubtless calculated securely on her being speedily driven back, as soon as the slender fund she had in her possession was expended, to throw herself unconditionally upon his tender mercies; and his disappointment in this expectation appears to have exasperated his feelings of resentment towards the poor woman, to a degree which few persons alive to the claims of common justice, not to speak of christianity or common humanity, could easily have anticipated. Such, at least, seems the only intelligible inference that can be drawn from his subsequent conduct.

The case having been submitted, by desire of the Anti-Slavery Committee,[2] to the consideration of Dr Lushington and Mr Sergeant Stephen,[3] it was found that there existed no legal means of compelling Mary's master to grant her manumission; and that if she returned to Antigua, she would inevitably fall again under his power, or that of his attorneys, as a slave. It was, however, resolved to try what could

be effected for her by amicable negotiation; and with this view Mr
Ravenscroft, a solicitor, (Mr G. Stephen's relative,) called upon Mr
Wood, in order to ascertain whether he would consent to Mary's
manumission on any reasonable terms, and to refer, if required, the
amount of compensation for her value to arbitration. Mr Ravenscroft
with some difficulty obtained one or two interviews, but found Mr
Wood so full of animosity against the woman, and so firmly bent
against any arrangement having her freedom for its object, that the
negotiation was soon broken off as hopeless. The angry slave-owner
declared 'that he would not move a finger about her in this country,
or grant her manumission on any terms whatever; and that if she went
back to the West Indies, she must take the consequences.'

This unreasonable conduct of Mr Wood, induced the Anti-Slavery
Committee, after several other abortive attempts to effect a compromise, to think of bringing the case under the notice of Parliament.[4]
The heads of Mary's statement were accordingly engrossed in a Petition, which Dr Lushington offered to present, and to give notice at
the same time of his intention to bring in a Bill to provide for the
entire emancipation of all slaves brought to England with the owner's
consent.[5] But before this step was taken, Dr Lushington again had
recourse to negociation with the master; and, partly through the
friendly intervention of Mr Manning,[6] partly by personal conference,
used every persuasion in his power to induce Mr Wood to relent and
let the bondwoman go free. Seeing the matter thus seriously taken
up, Mr Wood became at length alarmed, – not relishing, it appears,
the idea of having the case publicly discussed in the House of Commons; and to avert this result he submitted to temporize – assumed a
demeanour of unwonted civility, and even hinted to Mr Manning (as
I was given to understand) that if he was not driven to utter hostility
by the threatened exposure, he would probably meet our wishes 'in
his own time and way.' Having gained time by these manœuvres, he
adroitly endeavoured to cool the ardour of Mary's new friends, in her
cause, by representing her as an abandoned and worthless woman,
ungrateful towards him, and undeserving of sympathy from others;
allegations which he supported by the ready affirmation of some of
his West India friends, and by one or two plausible letters procured

from Antigua. By these and like artifices he appears completely to have imposed on Mr Manning, the respectable West India merchant whom Dr Lushington had asked to negotiate with him; and he prevailed so far as to induce Dr Lushington himself (actuated by the benevolent view of thereby best serving Mary's cause,) to abstain from any remarks upon his conduct when the petition was at last presented in Parliament. In this way he dexterously contrived to neutralize all our efforts, until the close of the Session[7] of 1829; soon after which he embarked with his family for the West Indies.

Every exertion for Mary's relief having thus failed; and being fully convinced from a twelvemonth's observation of her conduct, that she was really a well-disposed and respectable woman; I engaged her, in December 1829, as a domestic servant in my own family. In this capacity she has remained ever since; and I am thus enabled to speak of her conduct and character with a degree of confidence I could not have otherwise done. The importance of this circumstance will appear in the sequel.

From the time of Mr Wood's departure to Antigua, in 1829, till June or July last, no farther effort was attempted for Mary's relief. Some faint hope was still cherished that this unconscionable man would at length relent, and 'in his own time and way,' grant the prayer of the exiled negro woman. After waiting, however, nearly twelvemonths longer, and seeing the poor woman's spirits daily sinking under the sickening influence of hope deferred, I resolved on a final attempt in her behalf, through the intervention of the Moravian Missionaries, and of the Governor of Antigua. At my request, Mr Edward Moore, agent of the Moravian Brethren in London, wrote to the Rev. Joseph Newby, their Missionary in that island, empowering him to negotiate in his own name with Mr Wood for Mary's manumission, and to procure his consent, if possible, upon terms of ample pecuniary compensation. At the same time the excellent and benevolent William Allen, of the Society of Friends,[8] wrote to Sir Patrick Ross, the Governor of the Colony,[9] with whom he was on terms of friendship, soliciting him to use his influence in persuading Mr Wood to consent: and I confess I was sanguine enough to flatter myself that we should thus at length prevail. The result proved, however, that I had not yet fully appreciated the character of the man we had to deal with.

Mr Newby's answer arrived early in November last, mentioning that he had done all in his power to accomplish our purpose, but in vain; and that if Mary's manumission could not be obtained without Mr Wood's consent, he believed there was no prospect of its ever being effected.

A few weeks afterwards I was informed by Mr Allen, that he had received a letter from Sir Patrick Ross, stating that he also had used his best endeavours in the affair, but equally without effect. Sir Patrick at the same time inclosed a letter, addressed by Mr Wood to his Secretary, Mr Taylor, assigning his reasons for persisting in this extraordinary course. This letter requires our special attention. Its tenor is as follows:–

'My dear Sir,

'I reply to your note relative to the woman Molly, I beg you will have the kindness to oblige me by assuring his Excellency that I regret exceedingly my inability to comply with his request, which under other circumstances would afford me very great pleasure.

'There are many and powerful reasons for inducing me to refuse my sanction to her returning here in the way she seems to wish. It would be to reward the worst species of ingratitude, and subject myself to insult whenever she came in my way. Her moral character is very bad, as the police records will shew; and she would be a very troublesome character should she come here without any restraint. She is not a native of this country, and I know of no relation she has here. I induced her to take a husband,[10] a short time before she left this, by providing a comfortable house in my yard for them, and prohibiting her going out after 10 to 12 o'clock (our bed-time) without special leave. This she considered the greatest, and indeed the only, grievance she ever complained of, and all my efforts could not prevent it. In hopes of inducing her to be steady to her husband, who was a free man, I gave him the house to occupy during our absence; but it appears the attachment was too loose to bind her, and he has taken another wife: so on that score I do her no injury. In England she made her election, and quitted my family. This I had no right to object to; and I should have thought no more of it, but not satisfied to leave quietly, she gave every trouble and annoyance in her power, and endeavoured to injure the character of my family by the most vile and infamous falsehoods, which was embodied in a petition to the House of Commons, and would have been presented, had not my friends from this island, particularly the Hon. Mr Byam and Dr Coull, come forward, and disproved what she had asserted.

'It would be beyond the limits of an ordinary letter to detail her baseness, though I will do so should his Excellency wish it; but you may judge of her depravity by one circumstance, which came out before Mr Justice Dyett, in a quarrel with another female.[11]

*   *   *

'Such a thing I could not have believed possible.*

'Losing her value as a slave in a pecuniary point of view I consider of no consequence; for it was our intention, had she conducted herself properly and returned with us, to have given her freedom. She has taken her freedom; and all I wish is, that she would enjoy it without meddling with me.

'Let me again repeat, if his Excellency wishes it, it will afford me great pleasure to state such particulars of her, and which will be incontestably proved by numbers here, that I am sure will acquit me in his opinion of acting unkind or ungenerous towards her. I'll say nothing of the liability I should incur, under the Consolidated Slave Law,[12] of dealing with a free person as a slave.

'My only excuse for entering so much into detail must be that of my anxious wish to stand justified in his Excellency's opinion.

'I am, my dear Sir,

Yours very truly,

JOHN A. WOOD.

'*Charles Taylor, Esq.*   '*20th Oct.* 1830.'
   &c. &c. &c.

'I forgot to mention that it was at her own special request that she accompanied me to England – and also that she had a considerable sum of money with her, which she had saved in my service. I knew of £36 to £40, at least,

---

* I omit the circumstance here mentioned, because it is too indecent to appear in a publication likely to be perused by females. It is, in all probability, a vile calumny; but even if it were perfectly true, it would not serve Mr Wood's case one straw. – Any reader who wishes it may see the passage referred to, in the autograph letter in my possession. T. P.

for I had some trouble to recover it from a white man, to whom she had lent it.

'J.A.W.'

Such is Mr Wood's justification of his conduct in thus obstinately refusing manumission to the Negro-woman who had escaped from his 'house of bondage.'[13]

Let us now endeavour to estimate the validity of the excuses assigned, and the allegations advanced by him, for the information of Governor Sir Patrick Ross, in this deliberate statement of his case.

1. To allow the woman to return home free, would, he affirms 'be to reward the worst species of ingratitude.'

He assumes, it seems, the sovereign power of pronouncing a virtual sentence of banishment, for the alleged crime of ingratitude. Is this then a power which any man ought to possess over his fellow-mortal? or which any good man would ever wish to exercise? And, besides, there is no evidence whatever, beyond Mr Wood's mere assertion, that Mary Prince owed him or his family the slightest mark of gratitude. Her account of the treatment she received in his service, *may* be incorrect; but her simple statement is at least supported by minute and feasible details, and, unless rebutted by positive facts, will certainly command credence from impartial minds more readily than his angry accusation, which has something absurd and improbable in its very front. Moreover, is it not absurd to term the assertion of her *natural rights*[14] by a slave, – even supposing her to have been kindly dealt with by her 'owners,' and treated in every respect the reverse of what Mary affirms to have been her treatment by Mr Wood and his wife, – 'the *worst* species of ingratitude?' This may be West Indian ethics,[15] but it will scarcely be received as sound doctrine in Europe.

2. To permit her return would be 'to subject himself to insult whenever she came in his way.'

This is a most extraordinary assertion. Are the laws of Antigua then so favourable to the free blacks, or the colonial police so feebly administered, that there are no sufficient restraints to protect a rich colonist like Mr Wood, – a man who counts among his familiar friends the Honourable Mr Byam, and Mr Taylor the Government Secretary,

45

– from being insulted by a poor Negro-woman? It is preposterous.

3. Her moral character is so bad, that she would prove very troublesome should she come to the colony 'without any restraint.'

'Any restraint?' Are there no restraints (supposing them necessary) short of absolute slavery to keep 'troublesome characters' in order? But this, I suppose, is the *argumentum ad gubernatorem*[16] – to frighten the governor. She is such a termagant,[17] it seems, that if she once gets back to the colony *free*, she will not only make it too hot for poor Mr Wood, but the police and courts of justice will scarce be a match for her! Sir Patrick Ross, no doubt, will take care how he intercedes farther for so formidable a virago! How can one treat such arguments seriously?

4. She is not a native of the colony, and he knows of no relation she has there.

True: But was it not her home (so far as a slave can have a home) for thirteen or fourteen years? Were not the connexions, friendships, and associations of her mature life formed there? Was it not there she hoped to spend her latter years in domestic tranquillity with her husband, free from the lash of the taskmaster? These considerations may appear light to Mr Wood, but they are every thing to this poor woman.

5. He induced her, he says, to take a husband, a short time before she left Antigua, and gave them a comfortable house in his yard, &c. &c.

This paragraph merits attention. He 'induced her to take a husband?' If the fact were true, what brutality of mind and manners does it not indicate among these slave-holders? They refuse to legalize the marriages of their slaves, but *induce* them to form such temporary connexions as may suit the owner's conveniency, just as they would pair the lower animals;[18] and this man has the effrontery to tell us so! Mary, however, tells a very different story, (see page 17 [p. 30];) and her assertion, independently of other proof, is at least as credible as Mr Wood's. The reader will judge for himself as to the preponderance of internal evidence in the conflicting statements.

6. He alleges that she was, before marriage, licentious and even depraved in her conduct,[19] and unfaithful to her husband afterwards.

These are serious charges. But if true, or even partially true, how comes it that a person so correct in his family hours and arrangements as Mr Wood professes to be, and who expresses so edifying a horror of licentiousness, could reconcile it to his conscience to keep in the bosom of his family so *depraved*, as well as so *troublesome* a character for at least thirteen years, and confide to her for long periods too the charge of his house and the care of his children – for such I shall shew to have been the facts? How can he account for not having rid himself with all speed, of so disreputable an inmate – he who values her loss so little 'in a pecuniary point of view?' How can he account for having sold *five other slaves* in that period, and yet have retained this shocking woman – nay, even have refused to sell her, on more than one occasion, when offered her full value? It could not be from ignorance of her character, for the circumstance which he adduces as a proof of her shameless depravity, and which I have omitted on account of its indecency, occurred, it would appear, not less than *ten years ago*. Yet, notwithstanding her alleged ill qualities and habits of gross immorality, he has not only constantly refused to part with her; but after thirteen long years, brings her to England as an attendant on his wife and children, with the avowed intention of carrying her back along with his maiden daughter, a young lady returning from school! Such are the extraordinary facts; and until Mr Wood shall reconcile these singular inconsistencies between his actions and his allegations, he must not be surprised if we in England prefer giving credit to the former rather than the latter; although at present it appears somewhat difficult to say which side of the alternative is the more creditable to his own character.

7. Her husband, he says, has taken another wife; 'so that on that score,' he adds, 'he does her no injury.'

Supposing this fact be true, (which I doubt, as I doubt every mere assertion from so questionable a quarter,) I shall take leave to put a question or two to Mr Wood's conscience. Did he not write from England to his friend Mr Darrel, soon after Mary left his house, directing him to turn her husband, Daniel James, off his premises, on account of her offence; telling him to inform James at the same time that his wife had *taken up* with another man, who had robbed her of all she had – a calumny as groundless as it was cruel? I further ask if the person who invented this story (whoever he may be,) was not likely enough to impose similar fabrications on the poor negro man's credulity, until he may have been induced to prove false to his marriage vows, and to 'take another wife,' as Mr Wood coolly expresses it? But withal, I strongly doubt the fact of Daniel James's infidelity; for there is now before me a letter from himself to Mary, dated in April 1830, couched in strong terms of conjugal affection; expressing his anxiety for her speedy return, and stating that he had lately 'received a grace' (a token of religious advancement) in the Moravian church, a circumstance altogether incredible if the man were living in open adultery, as Mr Wood's assertion implies.

8. Mary, he says, endeavoured to injure the character of his family by infamous falsehoods, which were embodied in a petition to the House of Commons, and would have been presented, had not his friends from Antigua, the Hon. Mr Byam, and Dr Coull, disproved her assertions.

I can say something on this point from my own knowledge. Mary's petition contained simply a brief statement of her case, and, among other things, mentioned the treatment she had received from Mr and Mrs Wood. Now the principal facts are corroborated by other evidence, and Mr Wood must bring forward very different testimony from that of Dr Coull before well-informed persons will give credit to his contradiction. The value of that person's evidence in such cases will be noticed presently. Of the Hon. Mr Byam I know nothing, and shall only at present remark that it is not likely to redound greatly to his credit to appear in such company. Furthermore, Mary's petition *was* presented, as Mr Wood ought to know; though it was not discussed, nor his conduct exposed as it ought to have been.

9. He speaks of the liability he should incur, under the Consolidated Slave Law, of dealing with a free person as a slave.

Is not this pretext hypocritical in the extreme? What liability could he possibly incur by voluntarily resigning the power, conferred on him by an iniquitous colonial law,[20] of re-imposing the shackles of slavery on the bondwoman from whose limbs they had fallen when she touched the free soil of England? – There exists no liability from which he might not have been easily secured, or for which he would not have been fully compensated.

He adds in a postscript that Mary had a considerable sum of money with her, – from £36 to £40 at least, which she had saved in his service. The fact is, that she had at one time 113 dollars in cash; but only a very small portion of that sum appears to have been brought by her to England, the rest having been partly advanced, as she states, to assist her husband, and partly lost by being lodged in unfaithful custody.

Finally, Mr Wood repeats twice that it will afford him great pleasure to state for the governor's satisfaction, if required, such particulars of 'the woman Molly,' upon incontestable evidence, as he is sure will acquit him in his Excellency's opinion 'of acting unkind or ungenerous towards her.'

This is well: and I now call upon Mr Wood to redeem his pledge; – to bring forward facts and proofs fully to elucidate the subject; – to reconcile, if he can, the extraordinary discrepancies which I have pointed out between his assertions and the actual facts, and especially between his account of Mary Prince's character and his own conduct in regard to her. He has now to produce such a statement as will acquit him not only in the opinion of Sir Patrick Ross, but of the British public. And in this position he has spontaneously placed himself, in attempting to destroy, by his deliberate criminatory letter, the poor woman's fair fame and reputation, – an attempt but for which the present publication would probably never have appeared.

————

Here perhaps we might safely leave the case to the judgment of the public; but as this negro woman's character, not the less valuable to her because her condition is so humble, has been so unscrupulously blackened by her late master, a party so much interested and inclined to place her in the worst point of view, – it is incumbent on me, as her advocate with the public, to state such additional testimony in her behalf as I can fairly and conscientiously adduce.

My first evidence is Mr Joseph Phillips, of Antigua. Having submitted to his inspection Mr Wood's letter and Mary Prince's narrative, and requested his candid and deliberate sentiments in regard to the actual facts of the case, I have been favoured with the following letter from him on the subject:—

'London, January 18, 1831.

'Dear Sir,

'In giving you my opinions of Mary Prince's narrative, and of Mr Wood's letter respecting her, addressed to Mr Taylor, I shall first mention my opportunities of forming a proper estimate of the conduct and character of both parties.

'I have known Mr Wood since his first arrival in Antigua in 1803. He was then a poor young man, who had been brought up as a ship carpenter in Bermuda. He was afterwards raised to be a clerk in the Commissariat department, and realised sufficient capital to commence business as a merchant. This last profession he has followed successfully for a good many years, and is understood to have accumulated very considerable wealth. After he entered into trade, I had constant intercourse with him in the way of business; and in 1824 and 1825, I was regularly employed on his premises as his clerk; consequently, I had opportunities of seeing a good deal of his character both as a merchant and as a master of slaves. The former topic I pass over as irrelevant to the present subject: in reference to the latter, I shall merely observe that he was not, in regard to ordinary matters, more severe, probably, than the ordinary run of slave owners; but, if seriously offended, he was not of a disposition to be easily appeased, and was obstinate in adhering to any resolution he had once taken. As regards the exaction of work from domestic slaves, his wife was probably more severe than himself – it was almost impossible for the slaves ever to give her entire satisfaction.

'Of their slave Molly (or Mary) I know less than of Mr and Mrs Wood; but I saw and heard enough of her, both while I was constantly employed on Mr Wood's premises, and while I was there occasionally on business, to be quite certain that she was viewed by her owners as their most respectable and trustworthy female slave. It is within my personal knowledge that she had usually the charge of the house in their absence, was entrusted with the keys, &c.; and was always considered by the neighbours and visitors as their confidential household servant, and as a person in whose integrity they placed unlimited confidence, – although when Mrs Wood was at home, she was no doubt kept pretty closely at washing and other hard work. A decided proof of the estimation in which she was held by her owners exists in the fact that Mr Wood uniformly refused to part with her, whereas he sold five other slaves while she was with them. Indeed, she always appeared to me to be a slave of superior intelligence and respectability; and I always understood such to be her general character in the place.

'As to what Mr Wood alleges about her being frequently before the police, &c. I can only say I never heard of the circumstance before; and as I lived for twenty years in the same small town, and in the vicinity of their residence, I think I could scarcely have failed to become acquainted with it, had such been the fact. She might, however, have been occasionally before the magistrate in consequence of little disputes among the slaves, without any serious imputation on her general respectability. She says she was twice summoned to appear as a witness on such occasions; and that she was once sent by her mistress to be confined in the Cage,[21] and was afterwards flogged by her desire. This cruel practice is very common in Antigua; and, in my opinion, is but little creditable to the slave owners and magistrates by whom such arbitrary punishments are inflicted, frequently for very trifling faults. Mr James Scotland is the only magistrate in the colony who invariably refuses to sanction this reprehensible practice.

'Of the immoral conduct ascribed to Molly by Mr Wood, I can say nothing further than this – that I have heard she had at a former period (previous to her marriage) a connexion with a white person, a Capt. —,[22] which I have no doubt was broken off when she became seriously impressed with religion. But, at any rate, such connexions are so common, I might almost say universal, in our slave colonies, that except by the missionaries and a few serious persons, they are considered, if faults at all, so very venial as scarcely to deserve the name of immorality. Mr Wood knows this colonial estimate of such connexions as well as I do; and, however false such an estimate must be allowed to be, especially when applied to their own conduct by persons of education, pretending to adhere to the pure Christian rule of morals, – yet when he ascribes to a negro slave, to whom legal marriage was denied, such great criminality for laxity of this sort, and professes to be so exceedingly shocked and amazed at the tale he himself relates, he must, I am confident, have had a farther object in view than the information of Mr Taylor or Sir Patrick Ross. He must, it is evident, have been aware that his letter would be sent to Mr Allen, and accordingly adapted it, as more important documents from the colonies are often adapted, *for effect in England.* The tale of the slave Molly's immoralities, be assured, was not intended for Antigua so much as for Stoke Newington, and Peckham, and Aldermanbury.[23]

'In regard to Mary's narrative generally, although I cannot speak to the accuracy of the details, except in a few recent particulars, I can with safety declare that I see no reason to question the truth of a single fact stated by her, or even to suspect her in any instance of intentional exaggeration. It bears in my judgment the geniune stamp of truth and nature. Such is my unhesitating opinion, after a residence of twenty-seven years in the West Indies.
To T. Pringle, Esq.

'I remain, &c.
'JOSEPH PHILLIPS.'

'P.S. As Mr Wood refers to the evidence of Dr T. Coull in opposition to Mary's assertions, it may be proper to enable you justly to estimate the worth of that person's evidence in cases connected with the condition and treatment of slaves. You are aware that in 1829, Mr M'Queen of Glasgow,[24] in noticing a Report of the "Ladies' Society of Birmingham for the relief of British Negro Slaves,"[25] asserted with his characteristic audacity, that the statement which it contained respecting distressed and deserted slaves in Antigua was "an abominable falsehood." Not contented with this, and with insinuating that I, as agent of the society in the distribution of their charity in Antigua, had fraudulently duped them out of their money by a fabricated tale of distress, Mr M'Queen proceeded to libel me in the most opprobrious terms, as "a man of the most worthless and abandoned character."* Now I

---

* In elucidation of the circumstances above referred to, I subjoin the following extracts from the Report of the Birmingham Ladies' Society for 1830:–

'As a portion of the funds of this association has been appropriated to assist the benevolent efforts of a society which has for fifteen years afforded relief to distressed and deserted slaves in Antigua, it may not be uninteresting to our friends to learn the manner in which the agent of this society has been treated for simply obeying the command of our Saviour, by ministering, like the good Samaritan, to the distresses of the helpless and the desolate. The society's proceedings being adverted to by a friend of Africa, at one of the public meetings held in this country, a West Indian planter, who was present, wrote over to his friends in Antigua, and represented the conduct of the distributors of this charity in such a light, that it was deemed worthy of the cognizance of the House of Assembly. Mr Joseph Phillips, a resident of the island, who had most kindly and disinterestedly exerted himself in the distribution of the money from England among the poor deserted slaves, was brought before the Assembly,

know from good authority that it was *upon Dr Coull's information* that Mr M'Queen founded this impudent contradiction of notorious facts, and this audacious libel of my personal character. From this single circumstance you may judge of the value of his evidence in the case of Mary Prince. I can furnish

---

and most severely interrogated: on his refusing to deliver up his private correspondence with his friends in England, he was thrown into a loathsome jail,[a] where he was kept for nearly five months; while his loss of business, and the oppressive proceedings instituted against him, were involving him in poverty and ruin. On his discharge by the House of Assembly, he was seized in their lobby for debt, and again imprisoned.'

'In our report for the year 1826, we quoted a passage from the 13th Report of the Society for the relief of deserted Slaves in the island of Antigua, in reference to a case of great distress. This statement fell into the hands of Mr M'Queen, the Editor of the Glasgow Courier. Of the consequences resulting from this circumstance we only gained information through the Leicester Chronicle, which had copied an article from the Weekly Register of Antigua, dated St John's, September 22, 1829. We find from this that Mr M'Queen affirms, that "with the exception of the fact that the society is, as it deserves to be, duped out of its money, the whole tale" (of the distress above referred to) "is an abominable falsehood." This statement, which we are informed has appeared in many of the public papers, is COMPLETELY REFUTED in our Appendix, No. 4, to which we refer our readers. Mr M'Queen's statements, we regret to say, would lead many to believe that there are no deserted Negros to assist; and that the case mentioned was a perfect fabrication. He also distinctly avers, that the disinterested and humane agent of the society, Mr Joseph Phillips, is "a man of the most worthless and abandoned character." In opposition to this statement, we learn the good character of Mr Phillips from those who have long been acquainted with his laudable exertions in the cause of humanity, and from the Editor of the Weekly Register of Antigua, who speaks, on his own knowledge, of more than twenty years back; confidently appealing at the same time to the inhabitants of the colony in which he resides for the truth of his averments, and producing a testimonial to Mr Phillips's good character signed by two members of the Antigua House of Assembly, and by Mr Wyke, the collector of his Majesty's customs, and by Antigua merchants, as follows – "that they have been acquainted with him the last four years and upwards, and he has always conducted himself in an upright becoming manner – his character we know to be unimpeached, and his morals unexceptionable."

(Signed) 'Thomas Saunderson John D. Taylor
              John A. Wood George Wyke
              Samuel L. Darrel Giles S. Musson
                    Robert Grant.'

'St John's, Antigua, June 28, 1825.'

In addition to the above testimonies, Mr Phillips has brought over to England with him others of a more recent date, from some of the most respectable persons in Antigua – sufficient to cover with confusion all his unprincipled calumniators. See also his account of his own case in the Anti-Slavery Reporter, No. 74, p. 69.[b]

further information respecting Dr Coull's colonial proceedings, both private and judicial, should circumstances require it.'

'J.P.'

I leave the preceding letter to be candidly weighed by the reader in opposition to the inculpatory allegations of Mr Wood – merely remarking that Mr Wood will find it somewhat difficult to impugn the evidence of Mr Phillips, whose 'upright,' 'unimpeached,' and 'unexceptionable' character, he has himself vouched for in unqualified terms, by affixing his signature to the testimonial published in the Weekly Register of Antigua in 1825. (See Note below [above].)

The next testimony in Mary's behalf is that of Mrs Forsyth, a lady in whose service she spent the summer of 1829. – (See page 22 [p. 36].) This lady, on leaving London to join her husband, voluntarily presented Mary with a certificate, which, though it relates only to a recent and short period of her history, is a strong corroboration of the habitual respectability of her character. It is in the following terms:–

'Mrs Forsyth states, that the bearer of this paper (Mary James,)[26] has been with her for the last six months; that she has found her an excellent character, being honest, industrious, and sober; and that she parts with her on no other account than this – that being obliged to travel with her husband, who has lately come from abroad in bad health, she has no farther need of a servant. Any person wishing to engage her, can have her character in full from Miss Robson, 4, Keppel Street, Russel Square, whom Mrs Forsyth has requested to furnish particulars to any one desiring them.

'4, Keppel Street,[27] 28th Sept. 1829.'

In the last place, I add my own testimony in behalf of this negro woman. Independently of the scrutiny, which, as Secretary of the Anti-Slavery Society, I made into her case when she first applied for assistance, at 18, Aldermanbury, and the watchful eye I kept upon her conduct for the ensuing twelvemonths, while she was the occasional pensioner of the Society, I have now had the opportunity of closely observing her conduct for fourteen months, in the situation of a domestic servant in my own family; and the following is the deliberate opinion of Mary's character, formed not only by myself, but also by my wife and sister-in-law, after this ample period of observation. We have found her perfectly honest and trustworthy in all respects; so that we have no hesitation in leaving every thing in the house at her disposal. She had the entire charge of the house during our absence in Scotland for three months last autumn, and conducted herself in that charge with the utmost discretion and fidelity. She is not, it is true, a very expert housemaid, nor capable of much hard work, (for her constitution appears to be a good deal broken,) but she is careful, industrious, and anxious to do her duty and to give satisfaction. She is capable of strong attachments, and feels deep, though unobtrusive, gratitude for real kindness shown her. She possesses considerable natural sense, and has much quickness of observation and discrimination of character. She is remarkable for *decency* and *propriety* of conduct – and her *delicacy*, even in trifling minutiæ, has been a trait of special remark by the females of my family. This trait, which is obviously quite unaffected, would be a most inexplicable anomaly, if her former habits had been so indecent and depraved as Mr Wood alleges. Her chief faults, so far as we have discovered them, are, a somewhat violent and hasty temper, and a considerable share of natural pride and self-importance;[28] but these defects have been but rarely and transiently manifested, and have scarcely occasioned an hour's uneasiness at any time in our household. Her religious knowledge, notwithstanding the pious care of her Moravian instructors in Antigua, is still but very limited, and her views of christianity indistinct; but her profession, whatever it may have of imperfection, I am convinced, has nothing of insincerity. In short, we consider her on the whole as respectable and well-behaved a person in her station, as any domestic, white or black, (and we have had ample experience of both colours,) that we have ever had in our service.

But after all, Mary's character, important though its exculpation be to her, is not really the point of chief practical interest in this case. Suppose all Mr Wood's defamatory allegations to be true – suppose him to be able to rake up against her out of the records of the Antigua police, or from the veracious testimony of his brother colonists, twenty stories as bad or worse than what he insinuates – suppose the whole of her own statement to be false, and even the whole of her conduct since she came under our observation here to be a tissue of hypocrisy; – suppose all this – and leave the negro woman as black in character as in complexion,*[29] – yet it would affect not the main facts – which are these.

1. Mr Wood, not daring in England to punish this woman arbitrarily, as he would have done in the West Indies, drove her out of his house, or left her, at least, only the alternative of returning instantly to Antigua, with the certainty of severe treatment there, or submitting in silence to what she considered intolerable usage in his household.

2. He has since obstinately persisted in refusing her manumission, to enable her to return home in security, though repeatedly offered more than ample compensation for her value as a slave; and this on various frivolous pretexts, but really, and indeed not unavowedly, in order to *punish* her for leaving his service in England, though he himself had professed to give her that option. These unquestionable facts speak volumes.†

---

* If it even were so, how strong a plea of palliation might not the poor negro bring, by adducing the neglect of her various owners to afford religious instruction or moral discipline, and the habitual influence of their evil *example* (to say the very least,) before her eyes? What moral good could she possibly learn – what moral evil could she easily escape, while under the uncontrolled power of such masters as she describes Captain I— and Mr D— of Turk's Island? All things considered, it is indeed wonderful to find her such as she now is. But as she has herself piously expressed it, 'that God whom then she knew not mercifully preserved her for better things.'

† After the preceding pages were printed,' I was favoured with a communication from the Rev. J. Curtin,[d] to whom, among other acquaintances of Mr Wood's in this country, the entire proof sheets of this pamphlet had been sent for inspection. Mr Curtin, in reference to Mary Prince's narrative, as it regards himself, (see page 17 [p. 29],) states, 1. That sometime before her baptism, on her being admitted a catechumen,[e] preparatory to that holy ordinance, she brought a note from her owner, Mr Wood, recommending her for religious instruction, &c.; 2. That it was his usual practice, when any adult slaves came on *week days* to school, to require their owners' permission for their attendance; but that on *Sundays* the chapel was open indiscriminately to all. – Mary, however, after a personal interview with Mr Curtin, and after hearing his letter read by me, still maintains that Mr Wood's note recommended her for baptism merely, and that she never received any religious instruction whatever from Mr and Mrs Wood, or from any one else at that period beyond what she has stated in her narrative. In regard to her non-admission to the Sunday school without permission from her owners, she admits that she may possibly have mistaken the clergyman's meaning on that point, but says that such was certainly her impression at the time, and the actual cause of her non-attendance.

The case affords a most instructive illustration of the true spirit of the slave system, and of the pretensions of the slaveholders to assert, not merely their claims to a 'vested right' in the *labour* of their bondmen, but to an indefeasible property in them as their 'absolute chattels.'[30] It furnishes a striking practical comment on the assertions of the West Indians that self-interest is a sufficient check to the indulgence of vindictive feelings in the master; for here is a case where a man (a *respectable* and *benevolent* man as his friends aver,) prefers losing entirely the full price of the slave, for the mere satisfaction of preventing a poor black woman from returning home to her husband! If the pleasure

---

Mr Curtin finds in his books some reference to Mary's connection with a Captain —, (the individual, I believe, alluded to by Mr Phillips at page 32 [p. 51]); but he states that when she attended his chapel she was always decently and becomingly dressed, and appeared to him to be in a situation of trust in her mistress's family.

Mr Curtin offers no comment on any other part of Mary's statement; but he speaks in very favourable, though general terms of the respectability of Mr Wood, whom he had known for many years in Antigua; and of Mrs Wood, though she was not personally known to him, he says, that he had 'heard her spoken of by those of her acquaintance, as a lady of very mild and amiable manners.'

Another friend of Mr and Mrs Wood, a lady who had been their guest both in Antigua and England, alleges that Mary has grossly misrepresented them in her narrative, and says that she 'can vouch for their being the most benevolent, kind-hearted people that can possibly live.' She has declined, however, to furnish me with any written correction of the misrepresentations she complains of, although I offered to insert her testimony in behalf of her friends, if sent to me in time. And having already kept back the publication a fortnight waiting for communications of this sort, I will not delay it longer. Those who have withheld their strictures have only themselves to blame.

Of the general character of Mr and Mrs Wood, I would not designedly give any *unfair* impression. Without implicitly adopting either the view of Mary Prince, or the unmeasured encomiums of their West India partizans, I am willing to believe them to be, on the whole, fair specimens of colonial character. Let them even be rated, if their friends will have it so, in the most respectable class of slaveholders; and, laying every thing else entirely out of view, let Mr Wood's conduct in this affair be tried exclusively by the facts established beyond dispute, and by his own statement of the case in his letter to Mr Taylor. But then, I ask, if the very *best* and *mildest* of your slave-owners can act as Mr Wood is proved to have acted, what is to be expected of persons whose mildness, or equity, or common humanity no one will dare to vouch for? If such things are done in the green tree, what will be done in the dry?[f] – And what else then can Colonial Slavery possibly be, even in its best estate, but a system incurably evil and iniquitous? – I require no other data – I need add no further comment.

of thwarting the benevolent wishes of the Anti-Slavery Society in behalf of the deserted negro, be an additional motive with Mr Wood, it will not much mend his wretched plea.

———

I may here add a few words respecting the earlier portion of Mary Prince's narrative. The facts there stated must necessarily rest entirely, – since we have no collateral evidence, – upon their intrinsic claims to probability, and upon the reliance the reader may feel disposed, after perusing the foregoing pages, to place on her veracity. To my judgment, the internal evidence of the truth of her narrative appears remarkably strong. The circumstances are related in a tone of natural sincerity, and are accompanied in almost every case with characteristic and minute details, which must, I conceive, carry with them full conviction to every candid mind that this negro woman has actually seen, felt, and suffered all that she so impressively describes; and that the picture she has given of West Indian slavery is not less true than it is revolting.

But there may be some persons into whose hands this tract may fall, so imperfectly acquainted with the real character of Negro Slavery, as to be shocked into partial, if not absolute incredulity, by the acts of inhuman oppression and brutality related of Capt. I— and his wife, and of Mr D—, the salt manufacturer of Turk's Island. Here, at least, such persons may be disposed to think, there surely must be *some* exaggeration; the facts are too shocking to be credible. The facts are indeed shocking, but unhappily not the less credible on that account. Slavery is a curse to the oppressor scarcely less than to the oppressed: its natural tendency is to brutalize both. After a residence myself of six years in a slave colony,[31] I am inclined to doubt whether, as regards its *demoralizing* influence, the master is not even a greater object of compassion than his bondman. Let those who are disposed to doubt the atrocities related in this narrative, on the testimony of a sufferer, examine the details of many cases of similar barbarity that have lately come before the public, on unquestionable evidence. Passing over the reports of the Fiscal of Berbice,*[32] and the Mauritius horrors[33] recently

* See Anti-Slavery Reporter,[g] Nos. 5 and 16.

unveiled,* let them consider the case of Mr and Mrs Moss, of the Bahamas,[34] and their slave Kate, so justly denounced by the Secretary for the Colonies;† – the cases of Eleanor Mead,‡[35] – of Henry Williams,¶[36] – and of the Rev. Mr Bridges and Kitty Hylton,§ in Jamaica.[37] These cases alone might suffice to demonstrate the inevitable tendency of slavery as it exists in our colonies, to brutalize the master to a truly frightful degree – a degree which would often cast into the shade even the atrocities related in the narrative of Mary Prince; and which are sufficient to prove, independently of all other evidence, that there is nothing in the revolting character of the facts to affect their credibility; but that on the contrary, similar deeds are at this very time of frequent occurrence in almost every one of our slave colonies. The system of coercive labour may vary in different places; it may be more destructive to human life in the cane culture of Mauritius and Jamaica,[38] than in the predial[39] and domestic bondage of Bermuda or the Bahamas, – but the spirit and character of slavery are every where the same, and cannot fail to produce similar effects. Wherever slavery prevails, there will inevitably be found cruelty and oppression. Individuals who have preserved humane, and amiable, and tolerant dispositions towards their black dependents, may doubtless be found among slave-holders; but even where a happy instance of this sort occurs, such as Mary's first mistress, the kind-hearted Mrs Williams, the favoured condition of the slave is still as precarious as it is rare: it is every moment at the mercy of events; and must always be held by a tenure so proverbially uncertain as that of human prosperity, or human life. Such examples, like a feeble and flickering streak of light in a gloomy picture, only serve by contrast to exhibit the depth of the prevailing shades. Like other exceptions, they only prove the general rule: the unquestionable tendency of the system is to vitiate the best tempers, and to harden the most feeling hearts. 'Never be kind, nor speak kindly to a slave,' said an accomplished

* Ibid. No. 44.
† Ibid. No. 47.
‡ Ibid. No. 64, p. 345; No. 71, p. 481.
¶ Ibid. No. 65, p. 356; No. 69, p. 431; and No. 77.
§ Anti-Slavery Reporter, Nos. 66, 69, and 76.

English lady in South Africa to my wife: 'I have now,' she added, 'been for some time a slave-owner, and have found, from vexatious experience in my own household, that nothing but harshness and hauteur will do with slaves.'

I might perhaps not inappropriately illustrate this point more fully by stating many cases which fell under my own personal observation, or became known to me through authentic sources, at the Cape of Good Hope – a colony where slavery assumes, as it is averred, a milder aspect than in any other dependency of the empire where it exists; and I could shew, from the judicial records of that colony, received by me within these few weeks, cases scarcely inferior in barbarity to the worst of those to which I have just specially referred; but to do so would lead me too far from the immediate purpose of this pamphlet, and extend it to an inconvenient length. I shall therefore content myself with quoting a single short passage from the excellent work of my friend Dr Walsh, entitled 'Notices of Brazil,'[40] – a work which, besides its other merits, has vividly illustrated the true spirit of Negro Slavery, as it displays itself not merely in that country, but wherever it has been permitted to open its Pandora's box[41] of misery and crime.

Let the reader ponder on the following just remarks, and compare the facts stated by the Author in illustration of them, with the circumstances related at pages 6 and 7 [pp. 14–16] of Mary's narrative:–

'If then we put out of the question the injury inflicted on others, and merely consider the deterioration of feeling and principle with which it operates on ourselves, ought it not to be a sufficient, and, indeed, unanswerable argument, against the permission of Slavery?

'The exemplary manner in which the paternal duties are performed at home, may mark people as the most fond and affectionate parents; but let them once go abroad, and come within the contagion of slavery, and it seems to alter the very nature of a man; and the father has sold, and still sells, the mother and his children, with as little compunction as he would a sow and her litter of pigs; and he often disposes of them together.

'This deterioration of feeling is conspicuous in many ways among the Brazilians. They are naturally a people of a humane and good-natured disposition, and much indisposed to cruelty or severity of any kind. Indeed, the manner in which many of them treat their slaves is a proof of this, as it is really gentle and considerate; but the natural tendency to cruelty and oppression in the human heart, is continually evolved by the impunity and uncontrolled licence in which they are exercised. I never walked through the streets of Rio, that some house did not present to me the semblance of a bridewell,[42] where the moans and the cries of the sufferers, and the sounds of whips and scourges within, announced to me that corporal punishment was being inflicted. Whenever I remarked this to a friend, I was always answered that the refractory nature of the slave rendered it necessary, and no house could properly be conducted unless it was practised. But this is certainly not the case; and the chastisement is constantly applied in the very wantonness of barbarity, and would not, and dared not, be inflicted on the humblest wretch in society, if he was not a slave, and so put out of the pale of pity.

'Immediately joining our house was one occupied by a mechanic, from which the most dismal cries and moans constantly proceeded. I entered the shop one day, and found it was occupied by a saddler, who had two negro boys working at his business. He was a tawny, cadaverous-looking man, with a dark aspect; and he had cut from his leather a scourge like a Russian knout,[43] which he held in his hand, and was in the act of exercising on one of the naked children in an inner room: and this was the cause of the moans and cries we heard every day, and almost all day long.

'In the rear of our house was another, occupied by some women of bad character, who kept, as usual, several negro slaves. I was awoke early one morning by dismal cries, and looking out of the window, I saw in the back yard of the house, a black girl of about fourteen years old; before her stood her mistress, a white woman, with a large stick in her hand. She was undressed except her petticoat and chemise, which had fallen down and left her shoulders and bosom bare. Her hair was streaming behind, and every fierce and malevolent passion was depicted in her face. She too, like my hostess at Governo[44] [another striking illustration of the *dehumanizing* effects of Slavery,] was the very representation of a fury. She was striking the poor girl, whom she had driven up into a corner, where she was on her knees appealing for mercy. She shewed her none, but continued to strike her on the head and thrust the stick into her face, till she was herself exhausted, and her poor victim covered with blood. This scene was renewed every morning, and the cries and moans of the poor suffering blacks, announced that they were enduring the penalty of slavery, in being the objects on which the irritable and malevolent passions of the whites are allowed to vent themselves with impunity; nor could I help deeply deploring that state of society in which the vilest characters in the community are allowed an almost uncontrolled power of life and death, over their innocent, and far more estimable fellow-creatures.' – (Notices of Brazil, vol. ii. p. 354–356.)

In conclusion, I may observe that the history of Mary Prince furnishes a corollary to Lord Stowell's decision in the case of the slave Grace,[45] and that it is most valuable on this account. Whatever opinions may be held by some readers on the grave question of immediately abolishing Colonial Slavery, nothing assuredly can be more repugnant to the feelings of Englishmen than that the system should be permitted to extend its baneful influence to this country. Yet such is the case, when the slave landed in England still only possesses that qualified degree of freedom,[46] that a change of domicile will determine it. Though born a British subject, and resident within the shores of England, he is cut off from his dearest natural rights by the sad alternative of regaining them at the expence of liberty, and the certainty of severe treatment. It is true that he has the option of returning; but it is a cruel mockery to call it a voluntary choice, when upon his return depend his means of subsistence and his re-union with all that makes life valuable. Here he has tasted 'the sweets of freedom,' to quote the words of the unfortunate Mary Prince; but if he desires to restore himself to his family, or to escape from suffering and destitution, and the other evils of a climate uncongenial to his constitution and habits, he must abandon the enjoyment of his late-acquired liberty, and again subject himself to the arbitrary power of a vindictive master.

The case of Mary Prince is by no means a singular one; many of the same kind are daily occurring: and even if the case were singular, it would still loudly call for the interference of the legislature. In instances of this kind no injury can possibly be done to the owner by confirming to the slave his resumption of his natural rights. It is the master's spontaneous act to bring him to this country; he knows when he brings him that he divests himself of his property; and it is, in fact, a minor species of slave trading,[47] when he has thus enfranchised his slave, to *re-capture* that slave by the necessities of his condition, or by working upon the better feelings of his heart. Abstractedly from all legal technicalities, there is no real difference between thus compelling the return of the enfranchised negro, and trepanning[48] a free native of England by delusive hopes into perpetual slavery. The most ingenious casuist could not point out any essential distinction between the two cases. Our boasted liberty is the dream of imagination, and no longer the characteristic of our country, if its bulwarks can thus be thrown down by colonial special pleading. It would well become the character of the present Government to introduce a Bill into the Legislature making perpetual that freedom which the slave has acquired by his passage here, and thus to declare, in the most ample sense of the words, (what indeed we had long fondly believed to be the fact, though it now appears that we have been mistaken,) THAT NO SLAVE CAN EXIST WITHIN THE SHORES OF GREAT BRITAIN.

APPENDIX

[As inquiries have been made from various quarters respecting the existence of marks of severe punishment on Mary Prince's body, it seems proper to append to this Edition, the following letter on that subject, written by Mrs Pringle to Mrs Townsend, one of the benevolent Secretaries of the 'Birmingham Ladies' Society for Relief of Negro Slaves.']¹

'London, 7, Solly Terrace, Claremont Square,
March 28, 1831.

'Dear Madam,

'My husband having read to me the passage in your last letter to him, expressing a desire to be furnished with some description of the marks of former ill-usage on Mary Prince's person, – I beg in reply to state, that the whole of the back part of her body is distinctly scarred, and, as it were, *chequered*, with the vestiges of severe floggings. Besides this, there are many large scars on other parts of her person, exhibiting an appearance as if the flesh had been deeply cut, or lacerated with *gashes*, by some instrument wielded by most unmerciful hands. Mary affirms, that all these scars were occasioned by the various cruel punishments she has mentioned or referred to in her narrative; and of the entire truth of this statement I have no hesitation in declaring myself perfectly satisfied, not only from my dependence on her uniform veracity, but also from my previous observation of similar cases at the Cape of Good Hope.

'In order to put you in possession of such full and authentic evidence, respecting the marks on Mary Prince's person, as may serve your benevolent purpose in making the inquiry, I beg to add to my own testimony that of

Miss Strickland (the lady who wrote down in this house the narratives of Mary Prince and Ashton Warner),[2] together with the testimonies of my sister Susan and my friend Miss Martha Browne[3] – all of whom were present and assisted me this day in a second inspection of Mary's body.

> 'I remain, Dear Madam,
> 'Yours very truly,
> 'M. PRINGLE.'

'The above statement is certified and corroborated by

> 'SUSANNA STRICKLAND,
> 'SUSAN BROWN,
> 'MARTHA A. BROWNE.'

To
> Mrs Townsend,
> > West-Bromwich,
> > > Birmingham.

NARRATIVE OF LOUIS ASA-ASA,

A CAPTURED AFRICAN

THE following interesting narrative is a convenient supplement to the history of Mary Prince. It is given, like hers, as nearly as possible in the narrator's words, with only so much correction as was necessary to connect the story, and render it grammatical. The concluding passage in inverted commas, is entirely his own. While Mary's narrative shews the disgusting character of colonial slavery, this little tale explains with equal force the horrors in which it originates.

It is necessary to explain that Louis came to this country about five years ago, in a French vessel called the Pearl. She had lost her reckoning, and was driven by stress of weather into the port of St Ives, in Cornwall. Louis and his four companions were brought to London upon a writ of Habeas Corpus[1] at the instance of Mr George Stephen; and, after some trifling opposition on the part of the master of the vessel, were discharged by Lord Wynford.[2] Two of his unfortunate fellow-sufferers died of the measles at Hampstead;[3] the other two returned to Sierra Leone;[4] but poor Louis, when offered the choice of going back to Africa, replied, 'Me no father, no mother now; me stay with you.' And here he has ever since remained; conducting himself in a way to gain the good will and respect of all who know him. He is remarkably intelligent, understands our language perfectly, and can read and write well. The last sentences of the following narrative will seem almost too peculiar to be his own; but it is not the first time that in conversation with Mr George Stephen, he has made similar remarks. On one occasion in particular, he was heard saying to himself in the kitchen, while sitting by the fire apparently in deep thought, 'Me think, – me think –' A fellow-servant inquired what he meant; and he added,

'Me think what a good thing I came to England! Here, I know what God is, and read my Bible; in my country they have no God, no Bible.'

How severe and just a reproof of the guilty wretches who visit his country only with fire and sword! How deserved a censure upon the not less guilty men, who dare to vindicate the state of slavery, on the lying pretext, that its victims are of an inferior nature! And scarcely less deserving of reprobation are those who have it in their power to prevent these crimes, but who remain inactive from indifference, or are dissuaded from throwing the shield of British power over the victim of oppression, by the sophistry, and the clamour, and the avarice of the oppressor. It is the reproach and the sin of England. May God avert from our country the ruin which this national guilt deserves!

We lament to add, that the Pearl which brought these negroes to our shore, was restored to its owners at the instance of the French Government, instead of being condemned as a prize to Lieut. Rye, who, on his own responsibility, detained her, with all her manacles and chains and other detestable proofs of her piratical occupation on board. We trust it is not yet too late to demand investigation into the reasons for restoring her.

The Negro Boy's Narrative

My father's name was Clashoquin; mine is Asa-Asa. He lived in a country called Bycla, near Egie,[5] a large town. Egie is as large as Brighton; it was some way from the sea. I had five brothers and sisters. We all lived together with my father and mother; he kept a horse, and was respectable, but not one of the great men. My uncle was one of the great men at Egie: he could make men come and work for him: his name was Otou. He had a great deal of land and cattle. My father sometimes worked on his own land, and used to make charcoal. I was too little to work; my eldest brother used to work on the land; and we were all very happy.

A great many people, whom we called Adinyés,[6] set fire to Egie in the morning before daybreak; there were some thousands of them. They killed a great many, and burnt all their houses. They staid two days, and then carried away all the people whom they did not kill.[7]

They came again every now and then for a month, as long as they could find people to carry away. They used to tie them by the feet, except when they were taking them off, and then they let them loose; but if they offered to run away, they would shoot them. I lost a great many friends and relations at Egie; about a dozen. They sold all they carried away, to be slaves. I know this because I afterwards saw them as slaves on the other side of the sea. They took away brothers, and sisters, and husbands, and wives; they did not care about this. They were sold for cloth or gunpowder, sometimes for salt or guns; sometimes they got four or five guns for a man: they were English guns,[8] made like my master's that I clean for his shooting. The Adinyés burnt a great many places besides Egie. They burnt all the country wherever they found villages; they used to shoot men, women, and children, if they ran away.

They came to us about eleven o'clock one day, and directly they came they set our house on fire. All of us had run away. We kept together, and went into the woods, and stopped there two days. The Adinyés then went away, and we returned home and found every thing burnt. We tried to build a little shed, and were beginning to get comfortable again. We found several of our neighbours lying about wounded; they had been shot. I saw the bodies of four or five little children whom they had killed with blows on the head. They had carried away their fathers and mothers, but the children were too small for slaves, so they killed them. They had killed several others, but these were all that I saw. I saw them lying in the street like dead dogs.

In about a week after we got back, the Adinyés returned, and burnt all the sheds and houses they had left standing. We all ran away again; we went to the woods as we had done before. – They followed us the next day. We went farther into the woods, and staid there about four days and nights; we were half starved; we only got a few potatoes. My uncle Otou was with us. At the end of this time, the Adinyés found us. We ran away. They called my uncle to go to them; but he refused, and they shot him immediately: they killed him. The rest of us ran on, and they did not get at us till the next day. I ran up into a tree: they followed me and brought me down. They tied my feet. I do not know if they found my father and mother, and brothers and sisters: they had run faster than me, and were half a mile farther when I got up into the tree: I have never seen them since. – There was a man who ran up into the tree with me: I believe they shot him, for I never saw him again.

They carried away about twenty besides me. They carried us to the sea. They did not beat us: they only killed one man, who was very ill and too weak to carry his load: they made all of us carry chickens and meat for our food; but this poor man could not carry his load, and they ran him through the body with a sword. – He was a neighbour of ours. When we got to the sea they sold all of us, but not to the same person. They sold us for money; and I was sold six times over, sometimes for money, sometimes for cloth, and sometimes for a gun. I was about thirteen years old. It was about half a year from the time I was taken, before I saw the white people.

We were taken in a boat from place to place, and sold at every place we stopped at. In about six months we got to a ship, in which we first saw white people: they were French. They bought us. We found here a great many other slaves; there were about eighty, including women and children. The Frenchmen sent away all but five of us into another very large ship. We five staid on board till we got to England,[9] which was about five or six months. The slaves we saw on board the ship were chained together by the legs below deck, so close they could not move. They were flogged very cruelly: I saw one of them flogged till he died; we could not tell what for. They gave them enough to eat. The place they were confined in below deck was so hot and nasty I could not bear to be in it. A great many of the slaves were ill, but they were not attended to. They used to flog me very bad on board the ship: the captain cut my head very bad one time.

'I am very happy to be in England, as far as I am very well; – but I have no friend belonging to me, but God, who will take care of me as he has done already. I am very glad I have come to England, to know who God is. I should like much to see my friends again, but I do not now wish to go back to them: for if I go back to my own country, I might be taken as a slave again. I would rather stay here, where I am free, than go back to my country to be sold. I shall stay in England as long as (please God) I shall live. I wish the King of England could know all I have told you. I wish it that he may see how cruelly we are used. We had no king in our country, or he would have stopt it. I think the king of England might stop it, and this is why I wish him to know it all. I have heard say he is good; and if he is, he will stop it if he can. I am well off myself, for I am well taken care of, and have good bed and good clothes; but I wish my own people to be as comfortable.'

NOTES

THE HISTORY OF MARY PRINCE

1. *the Supplement*: the editor, Thomas Pringle's Supplement, reprinted after the *History*.

2. *by a lady*: Susanna Strickland (1803–85), later Moodie, who wrote down Prince's *History*. *The Dictionary of National Biography* describes Strickland as an 'authoress' and wife of John Wedderburn Dunbar Moodie, a lieutenant in the Royal North British Fusiliers who spent ten years in South Africa. Strickland published numerous works including *Enthusiasm and Other Poems* (1831) and novels such as *The World Before Them* (1868) which was described by one reviewer as 'the handiwork of a sensible, amiable, refined and very religious lady'. The *DNB* does not mention Strickland's connection with the Anti-Slavery Society.

3. *Mr Joseph Phillips*: resident of Antigua and opponent of slavery, clerk of the Anti-Slavery Society. Phillips was the author of *The Outline of a Plan for the Total, Immediate and Safe Abolition of Slavery Throughout the British Colonies* (London, 1833) in which he calls for the abolition of enslavement by 1 July 1834, the abolition of corporal punishment in the colonies, a system of indenture for ex-slaves, universal employment, fixed working hours and the payment of wages to newly freed workers. He was imprisoned in Antigua for his activities on behalf of the Anti-Slavery Society: see 'Supplement', notes 25 and b, pp. 83 and 86.

4. *the Anti-Slavery Society*: founded in 1823, its leading members were William Wilberforce, Thomas Clarkson, Zachary Macaulay and James Stephen the Elder. It was not the first organized campaign against slavery in Britain: in 1787, William Wilberforce, acting on prime minister William Pitt's suggestion, formed the Committee for the Abolition of the Slave Trade, and in 1831 radical members of the Anti-Slavery Society broke away to form the Agency Anti-Slavery Society. Thomas Pringle was appointed secretary of the Anti-Slavery Society in 1827.

5. *Mr George Stephen*: the solicitor consulted by Pringle on Prince's behalf.

Stephen also represented Pringle in the libel case that he brought against the publisher Thomas Cadell in February 1833. See 'Supplement', note 24, p. 82, and Introduction, 'The *History* and Libel Cases'.

6. *the interesting narrative of Asa-Asa*: reprinted at the end of the *History*, after Thomas Pringle's Supplement.

7. *Tho. Pringle*: Thomas Pringle (1789–1834), editor of *The History of Mary Prince*, Scottish poet and secretary of the Anti-Slavery Society from 1827 until his death in 1834. A contribution to James Hogg's *Poetic Mirror* in 1816 brought Pringle the friendship of Walter Scott, who assisted him when he decided to emigrate to South Africa in 1820 because of straitened circumstances. However, Pringle fell foul of the colonial authorities in South Africa when the two journals he established were suppressed by the governor, and he returned to London in 1826. In October 1826 he published an article on the slave trade in the *New Monthly Magazine*, a similar article appearing in the *Anti-Slavery Monthly Reporter* on 31 January 1827 (see Appendix Four). His account of the 'misery and degradation' of South African slavery brought Pringle to the attention of prominent Abolitionist campaigners Zachary Macaulay and William Wilberforce, and led to his appointment as secretary of the Anti-Slavery Society. His *African Sketches* (including his 'Narrative of a Residence in South Africa', published separately in 1835) was published in 1834, and it includes the poem 'Afar in the Desert', which Coleridge described as 'among the two or three most perfect lyric poems in our language'. Pringle first met Mary Prince in 1828 when she came to the headquarters of the Anti-Slavery Society in Aldermanbury, east London, and in 1829 he and his wife employed her as a domestic servant in their own household where she remained until at least 1833 (see Pringle's Supplement).

8. SECOND EDITION: I have not been able to locate the second edition. Copies of the first and third editions of the text are in Rhodes House, Oxford, and the British Library.

9. *'the stranger . . . within our gates'*: Deuteronomy 14: 21: 'Ye shall not eat of any thing that dieth of itself, thou shalt give it unto the stranger that *is* in thy gates, that he may eat it; or thou mayest sell it unto an alien.' See also Deuteronomy 5: 14, Exodus 20: 10.

10. *Brackish-Pond, in Bermuda*: Bermuda, a group of islands in the North Atlantic Ocean covering only twenty-one square miles, has been a British Crown Colony since 1684. The first slaves were introduced into the islands in 1616, and they were mainly Africans and Native Americans who were put to work as servants, construction workers and sailors. In 1834, when the slaves were emancipated, out of a population of 9,000, nearly 5,000 were listed on the census as 'black' or 'coloured'. Bermuda is divided into parishes which were named after the stockholders of the Virginia Company, the original colonizers of the island. Brackish Pond is in the parish of Devonshire.

11. *Crow-Lane*: a street in the city of Hamilton, the capital of Pembroke parish.

12. *household slave*: a slave who did not work on the plantations.

13. *in the adjoining parish*: parish of Pembroke to the east of Devonshire parish where Mary Prince was born.

14. *it was according to my strength*: see Joshua 14: 11: 'as my strength *was* then, even so *is* my strength now'.

15. *'Here comes one of my poor picanninies!'*: *The Oxford English Dictionary* glosses *piccanniny* as 'a little one', 'a child'; the term (which now gives offence when used by people of European extraction) refers in the Caribbean and American to people of black African ethnic origin; in South and Central America to aboriginal peoples.

16. *osnaburgs*: a kind of coarse linen originally made in Osnabruck, a town in North Germany.

17. *Hamble Town*: Hamilton, the capital city of the parish of Pembroke.

18. *cayenne*: pungent powder obtained from the dried and ground pods and seeds of various species of capsicum from southern America.

19. *vendue master*: the organizer of a slave market (a vendue is a public sale or auction). In *The Interesting Narrative of Olaudah Equiano, or Gustavus Vassa, the African, Written by Himself* (London, 1794; ed. Vincent Caretta, New York: Penguin, 1995), Olaudah Equiano describes the horrors of the slave market where he was put up for sale in Barbados. 'In this manner, without scruple, are relations and friends separated, most of them never to see each other again,' he writes, and he rebukes 'nominal Christians' for their inhumane treatment of Africans (p. 60). His sense of outrage here is more palpable than Mary Prince's. Thomas Pringle also describes a slave market in his poem 'The Bechuana Boy' (see Appendix One).

20. *Spanish Point*: in the parish of Pembroke, at the westernmost tip of the island.

21. *a French Black*: i.e. from one of the French colonies in Africa.

22. *privateering*: a privateer is an armed vessel owned and commanded by private persons holding a commission from a government authorizing its owners to use it against a hostile nation, especially in the capture of merchant shipping.

23. *a mulatto, called Cyrus*: Cyrus the Elder (559–529 BC) was the founder of the Persian Empire, and Cyrus the Younger (*c.* 430–401 BC) held high command in Asia Minor during the Peloponnesian War. In one of his footnotes to the *History*, Pringle notes the planters' custom of giving slaves exaggeratedly grand

or dignified names, presumably as a means of humiliation. See Equiano's *Interesting Narrative* (p. 64) for a description of his renaming and his refusal at first to take the name of Gustavus Vasa of Sweden.

24. *Guinea*: country on the west coast of Africa.

25. *licks*: blows with a whip.

26. *during her pregnancy*: sexual relations between male slave owners and female slaves were common. Mary Prince does not give the details of Hetty's pregnancy, nor does she describe her own sexual relations with her subsequent master Mr D—, although it is possible to infer this from her narrative. In evidence given at the libel case which Wood brought against Pringle in March 1833, Prince says that she lived with a Captain Abbot for seven years, and their relationship was obviously a sexual one, for when Prince found another woman in bed with him she 'licked' (whipped) her. Prince left the Moravian Society because of her liaison with Abbot, and she also says that she lived with a freeman, Oyskman, who promised to make her free. She says that she narrated all these details to Susanna Strickland, but they were not written down. See *The Times*, 1 March 1833 (reprinted in Appendix Three). Such censorship was probably a concession to the moral sensibilities of Christian readers of the *History*, and in her edition of the *History* (London: Pandora, 1987, p. 3) Moira Ferguson suggests that Prince 'encodes' her sexual experience in order to foster the impression that she is pure, Christian and innocent. Mary Prince's *History* contrasts in this respect with the African-American Harriet Jacobs' *Incidents in the Life of a Slave Girl* (1861), which is much more sexually explicit.

27. *sweet-potatoe slips*: possibly a soft, semi-liquid mass made of sweet potatoes, from 'slop', semi-liquid food of a weak unappetizing kind.

28. *the salt-water channel*: a channel cut so that salt could be collected in the salt pans.

29. *sloop*: a small, one-masted vessel.

30. *Turk's Island*: the Turks and Caicos Islands lie 900 miles south east of Bermuda, 575 miles south east of Miami, Florida, directly east of Inagua at the southernmost tip of the Bahamas, and north of Hispaniola. They consist of two groups of about forty low-lying islands and cays (sand banks) covering 193 square miles and surrounded by one of the longest coral reefs in the world. The Turks Islands consist of two inhabited islands, Grand Turk and Salt Cay, six inhabited cays and a large number of rocks (see Paul G. Boultbee, *Turks and Caicos Islands*, Oxford: Clio Press, 1991). It is probable that when Prince refers to 'Turks Island', she is talking about Grand Turk.

Apparently named after the giant 'turk's head' cactus which grows there, the islands were 'discovered' in 1512. European salt-rakers were the first to inhabit the islands, establishing plantations there and only leaving the area after Abolition in the 1830s. In the early eighteenth century, both the Bahamians and the Bermudans asserted their rights to the Turks and Caicos Islands, but Bermuda was prevented from colonizing the islands because of its own status as a colony. The islanders resisted Bahamian attempts at integration, but at the beginning of the nineteenth century the islands were incorporated into the Bahamas colony. The Turks and Caicos Islands became a separate colony in 1848. For a contemporary description of the islands see Daniel McKinnen, *A Tour Through the British West Indies, in the Years 1802 and 1803* (London, 1804), pp. 121–9.

31. *the Buckra people*: the *OED* identifies the word as deriving from Black patois of Surinam, *backra*, master, and glosses it as 'white man (in Black speech)'.

32. *Grand Quay*: Prince means Grand Turk, the largest inhabited island of the Turks and Caicos Islands (see note 30, above). It is unclear, though, which settlement she means when she refers (two lines later) to the 'small town' of Grand Quay.

33. *the salt ponds*: The salt industry remained the economic mainstay of the Turks Islands until the 1960s. In the eighteenth century imported slaves were put to work raking in the salt ponds, and the harvested salt was then traded north up the American coast in return for money and food. Daniel McKinnen gives the following description of the salt industry in the Turks Islands:

Early in the year, when the power of the sun begins to increase, accompanied with dry weather, the salt every where in these natural ponds begins to crystallize and subside in solid cakes. It remains then only to break the crystals, and rake the salt on shore; and by this easy mode a single labourer may rake from forty to sixty bushels of salt in a day. The process, however, is facilitated by making small pans, which as the salt is taken out, may be replenished with brine from the pond [McKinnen, 124].

See also Howard Johnson's *The Bahamas in Slavery and Freedom* (Kingston, Jamaica; Randle Publishers, 1991), which contains the following contemporary description of salt-raking on the Turks Islands by Governor John Gregory which corroborates Prince's account of her pain and discomfort:

It must be borne in mind that the labour of salt-raking is most distasteful to the Negro; as well as the White man, involving the most painful Exposure of the face to the Sun and Mosquitoes and the most distressing Effects upon the feet from constant immersion in brine. In fact, no man will voluntarily submit to it, Except under the stimulus of very high wages [Johnson, 74–5].

34. *Indian corn*: maize.

35. *trusses*: bundles of hay or straw.

36. *the diving season*: i.e. diving for stones in the manner Prince has just described.

37. *South Creek*: an area in the south of Grand Turk island, comprising lagoons and red mangroves.

38. *large bills, to cut up mangoes to burn lime with*: the 'bills' Prince refers to here may have been hoes or chopping instruments, and mangoes were evidently used as fuel with which to burn limestone to produce lime or quick lime, which was used in the manufacture of mortar or cement, or as a manure.

39. *the overseer of the slaves*: a superintendent of the slaves.

40. *prickly-pear bushes*: prickly pear is a cactus with edible pear-shaped fruit.

41. *a sloop . . . loaded with slaves to work in the salt water*: slaves from Bermuda were shipped to the Turks Islands to rake salt.

42. *plantains*: long, pod-shaped, cucumber-like fleshy fruit, closely allied to the banana (*OED*).

43. *Cedar Hills*: Prince may be referring to what is now Cedar Grove, a town in the north of the island.

44. *Antigua*: one of the Windward Islands, located between the Atlantic and the Caribbean. 'Discovered' in 1493 by Columbus, it was settled by British people from St Christopher's in 1632, and after a brief French occupation between 1666 and 1667 it became a British colony. In 1671 it became one of the newly created Leeward Islands until the formation of the West India Federation in 1958. For contemporary descriptions of the island, see Mrs Flanighan, *Antigua and the Antiguans; a Full Account of the Colony and Its Inhabitants from the Time of the Caribs to the Present Day*, 2 vols (London, 1844), Bryan Edwards, *The History, Civil and Commercial, of the British West Indies*, 5 vols, 5th edn (London, 1819) and Daniel McKinnen, *A Tour Through the British West Indies*. According to McKinnen, in 1774 the population was estimated at 2,590 white people and 37,808 slaves, while in 1787 the figures had increased to 5,000 white people and 45,000 'negroes and people of colour' (although he thinks that the latter might be an over-estimate; see McKinnen, 75).

45. *the town of St John's*: the capital of Antigua, on the north-west coast of the island. The town is on a hill, and according to McKinnen's estimate at the beginning of the nineteenth century it contained around 1,800 houses.

46. *about fifteen years ago*: i.e. when Mary Prince was twenty-eight years old.

47. *Saint Anthony's fire*: the entry in the *Encyclopaedia Britannica* of 1773 describes erysipelas or St Anthony's fire as an eruptive fever which may affect any part of the body but which usually attacks the face (Prince tells us that her leg is affected). Symptoms include chilliness, shivering and fever, the body part swells up into red pustules and blisters which eventually turn yellow or black and blue. It is a serious, sometimes fatal, condition as the affected body part can turn gangrenous, and a leg may swell to three times its normal size. Cures include blood letting and administering purging potions, and the *Encyclopaedia* advises the patient to consume water-gruel, barley broth and roasted apples (*Encyclopaedia Britannica*, 3 vols, 1773, vol. III, 'Medicine', 'Of the Erysipelas, or St. Anthony's Fire').

48. *the Cage*: the *OED* describes this as a 'prison for petty malefactors; a lock-up (obs.)'.

49. *a quarrel I had about a pig with another slave woman*: Prince mentions this quarrel in her evidence at the libel trial against Pringle: 'Witness was ... before the justice about beating a female slave, respecting a pig. Witness did not beat the woman, but she was punished as though she did.' See *The Times*, 1 March 1833 (Appendix Three).

50. *the Point*: located on the coast of St John's, on the bay.

51. *cooper*: craftsman who makes and repairs wooden vessels (e.g. barrels).

52. *Captain Abbot*: in the evidence that she gave at the libel trial against Pringle in March 1833, Prince claimed that she lived with Captain Abbot for seven years, although apparently '[s]he did not live in the house with him, but slept with him sometimes in another hut'. See *The Times*, 1 March 1833 (Appendix Three).

53. *salt fish*: dried fish preserved in salt.

54. *shad barrels*: barrels used for storing fish.

55. *marshal*: an officer in a court of law.

56. *a Methodist meeting*: Methodism, the Christian sect founded by John and Charles Wesley at Oxford in 1729, was an evangelistic movement led by the Wesleys and George Whitfield. Like the Moravians, they had a strong missionary project, and John Wesley published an early Abolitionist polemic, *Thoughts Upon Slavery*, in 1774. Methodism was first established in Antigua in 1760 by Nathaniel Gilbert, who had met John Wesley in England. John Baxter, a shipwright from England, was another prominent Methodist who revived the community when he arrived in Antigua in 1778. He supervised the building of a Methodist chapel in St John's in which he preached his first sermon in 1783. In 1788 there were 2,000 members of the society, and by 1802 this figure had doubled. After Baxter's death in 1805, Methodism spread to other Caribbean islands, although Antigua continued to be regarded as the parent island. 'Thus,' writes Mrs Flanighan, 'from a small beginning – from a few black slaves gathered together by night beneath the roof of a white man – this society has spread far and wide, like some huge wave, until now it boasts a vast increase of number, of every variety and shade, from the ruddy sons of Britain, down to the jetty offspring of Afric's soil' (I: 240–48).

57. *a black driver*: a black slave driver.

58. *Moravian church*: A Protestant sect established in Lusitania, Upper Saxony, which has been called the first international Protestant church. The Moravians were descendants of Unitas Fratrum, the Church of Bohemian Brethren founded by a group of Hussites from 1457 and suppressed in Bohemia and Moravia in the 1620s (see Introduction).

In his *Narrative of a Residence in South Africa* (London, 1835), Thomas Pringle describes the ordered lifestyle of Moravian missionaries, but he comments on 'the peculiar and rather monastic regulations which are observed in their European establishments'. Mrs Flanighan describes the growing popularity of the Moravian mission in Antigua in the eighteenth century, and she comments also on the simplicity and openness of the Moravians (I: 254–61 and Introduction). However, Eric Williams points out that '[t]he Moravian missionaries in the islands held slaves without hesitation'. See *Capitalism and Slavery* (Chapel Hill: University Press of North Carolina, 1994), p. 43.

59. *I followed the church earnestly every opportunity*: religious conversion and spiritual regeneration are stock features of eighteenth-century slave narratives such as Olaudah Equiano's *Interesting Narrative* and Ukawsaw Gronniosaw's *Narrative of the Most Remarkable Particulars in the Life of James Albert Ukawsaw Gronniosaw, an African Prince, As Related By Himself* (c. 1770, Leeds, 1810). Mary Prince emphasizes her religious conversion, possibly because the widespread (and mistaken) belief that baptism would set a slave free may still have persisted in England at the beginning of the nineteenth century. See Peter Fryer, *Staying Power. The History of Black People in Britain* (London: Pluto Press, 1984), pp. 114–15.

60. *We were joined in marriage . . . by the Rev. Mr Olufsen*: there is no record of Mary Prince's marriage to Daniel James in the 'Spring Gardens Banns of Marriage 1826' at the Moravian Archive in Bethlehem, Pennsylvania, but a 'J. Olufsen' was the officiating minister at a marriage between two slaves, 'Elias and Amy', on 13 September 1827, which would seem to corroborate the details Prince gives here. The unusual spelling of Olufsen in both the 'Spring Gardens Marriage Banns 1827–1834' and in Prince's *History* might suggest that she had a marriage certificate from which she or Pringle misread the name. However, the petition presented to Parliament in 1829 states that Prince and James were married by a Moravian minister called Mr Ellensen (see Appendix Two).

Spring Gardens Moravian church in St John's, Antigua, is still located on St John's Street. In *Antigua and the Antiguans*, Mrs Flanighan gives the following description of the church: 'The settlement of St John's is situated in Spring Gardens, at the extreme north end of the town, and looks the very picture of neatness and domestic comfort. The present chapel, erected in 1773, is a plain building, devoid of any great architectural beauty, it is true, but interesting from its very simplicity, and from being built by the negroes in times of slavery' (I: 250).

61. *English marriage*: prohibited to slaves in the Anglican church, but permitted in non-conformist churches.

62. *the Tower*: i.e. the Tower of London.

63. *Leigh Street*: in Bloomsbury, central London, near Tavistock Square and Gordon Square.

64. *brig*: slave ship, a vessel with two masts.

65. *I was free in England*: Mary Prince is aware of her legal rights: under English law, slaves were free as long as they remained in England, but they resumed their slave status as soon as they returned to the colonies. See Introduction, 'The Black Community and the Law'.

66. *bed-ticks*: large, flat, quadrangular bag or case stuffed with feathers, hair, straw, chaff, etc. to form a mattress.

67. *black the shoes*: i.e. polish the shoes.

68. *Hatton Garden*: in central London, between High Holborn and Clerkenwell, parallel to Gray's Inn Road. The Wesleyan Missionary Society was located at 77 Hatton Garden.

69. *a gentleman who inquired into my case*: i.e. Thomas Pringle.

70. *to eat the bread of idleness*: Proverbs 31: 27: 'She looketh well to the ways of her household, and eateth not the bread of idleness.'

71. *charwoman*: woman hired to do odd jobs and cleaning in the household.

72. *Margate*: on the north coast of Kent, near Canterbury.

73. *gave me a good character*: i.e. a reference, which Pringle includes in his Supplement.

74. *found coals and candle*: i.e. provided her own heating and lighting.

75. *absent in Scotland*: Thomas Pringle and his wife Margaret were both Scottish.

76. *Miss S—*: Susanna Strickland.

77. *done up*: (colloquial) finished, exhausted.

78. *the great King of England*: King William IV (1830–37). Eric Williams notes that 'the royal Duke of Clarence, the future William IV, "took up the cudgills" against abolition and attacked Wilberforce as either a fanatic or a hypocrite' in 1793. George III was also an opponent of abolition. See Williams, 39.

Notes on the Footnotes

a. *the following description . . . published by me in 1826*: Pringle is referring to his article on the South African slave trade published in the *New Monthly Magazine* (see note 7, above). The extract Pringle includes here is taken from a letter he received from a friend.

b. *at a Veld-Cornet's*: i.e. field-cornet, 'the magistrate of a township in Cape Colony' (*OED*).

c. *Mrs Trimmer's 'Charity School Spelling Book'*: Sarah Trimmer (1741–1810), educational and children's writer, and the author of instructive and religious works, including *The Charity School Spelling Book . . . in Words of One Syllable Only*, 5th edn (1799).

d. *the Anti-Slavery Office in Aldermanbury*: headquarters of the Anti-Slavery Society in east London, off Cheapside.

e. *Mr George Stephen*: see note 5, above.

f. *the whole of this paragraph . . . Mary's precise words*: there is a notable shift in register from this point onwards, and the contrast gives an indication of the grammatical and syntactical interventions Pringle may have made in editing Mary Prince's narrative.

g. *West Indians*: i.e. white West Indians. For examples of the sort of anti-Abolition polemic to which Prince may be referring, see Edward Long, *The History of Jamaica: or, a General Survey of the Antient and Modern State of that Island*, 3 vols (London, 1774), and his *Candid Reflections Upon the Judgement Lately Awarded . . . on what is commonly called the Negroe-Cause, by a Planter* (London, 1772).

SUPPLEMENT TO THE HISTORY OF MARY PRINCE

1. *THE EDITOR*: Thomas Pringle.

2. *the Anti-Slavery Committee*: see Introduction, 'The Anti-Slavery Society and Thomas Pringle', Reginald Coupland, *The British Anti-Slavery Movement* (London: Butterworth, 1933), p. 137, and Christine Bolt, *The Anti-Slavery Movement and Reconstruction. A Study of Anglo-American Co-operation 1833–77* (Oxford: Oxford University Press, 1969), p. 5.

3. *Dr Lushington and Mr Sergeant Stephen*: Stephen Lushington (1782–1873), Member of Parliament and reformer. The *DNB* records that in March 1824 Lushington supported the introduction of Canning's bill for the 'more effectual suppression of the African Slave trade', and on 12 June 1827 he presented several petitions from 'people of colour in the West Indies' and urged that they be given full legal protection. Sir James Stephen (1789–1850) ('Sergeant' in this context means lawyer) was the colonial under-secretary responsible for drawing up the Abolition Bill of 1833. He was a regular contributor to the *Edinburgh Review*, and his first article in April 1838 was on William Wilberforce.

4. *bringing the case under the notice of Parliament*: a petition was presented to Parliament on Mary Prince's behalf of 24 June 1829. See Appendix Two for a report.

5. *a Bill . . . with the owner's consent*: See Introduction, 'The Black Community and the Law', for existing law.

6. *Mr Manning*: Mr Manning gave evidence at the libel trial in March 1833, where he 'stated that he had a correspondence with the plaintiff [i.e. Wood] respecting Mary Prince. The plaintiff was disposed, on certain conditions, to manumit her, but did not wish to be driven to it by the interference of others' (*The Times*, 1 March 1833).

7. *the Session*: the parliamentary session or term.

8. *William Allen, of the Society of Friends*: William Allen (1770–1843), philanthropist, scientist and lifelong member of the Quaker movement. Interested from boyhood in the movement to abolish the slave trade, he became friends with prominent abolitionists Thomas Clarkson and William Wilberforce in the 1790s. After the abolition of the slave trade he became an active member of the African Institution, continuing the campaign to abolish slavery.

9. *Sir Patrick Ross, the Governor of the Colony*: Mrs Flanighan's *Antigua and the Antiguans* gives the following account of Ross: 'Sir Benjamin D'Urban being recalled, Sir Patrick Ross was appointed governor and commander-in-chief. His excellency arrived in Antigua in the year 1826, and during his stay there, ingratiated himself with the *heads of the island*, by his courteous manners, and his humane desire to spare their feelings upon the all-engrossing topic of approaching emancipation' (I: 146). It was indeed a turbulent time on the island, and Flanighan reports a 'negro insurrection' in 1831, a year before Ross retired as governor.

10. *I induced her to take a husband*: this of course directly contradicts Prince's account of her marriage.

11. *a quarrel with another female*: Wood is referring to the dispute described by Prince in the evidence she gave at the libel trial of March 1833. See Introduction, 'The History and Libel Cases'.

12. *the Consolidated Slave Law*: parliamentary acts passed in the late eighteenth and early nineteenth centuries affirmed the need 'to consolidate and amend all the laws relating to slaves'. See Hansard, *Parliamentary Debates*, vol. XV (1827), pp. 1284–1366.

13. *'house of bondage'*: Exodus 13: 3: 'And Moses said unto the people, Remember this day, in which ye came out from Egypt, out of the house of bondage.'

14. *the assertion of her natural rights*: the OED glosses 'natural rights' as the doctrines in Western political philosophy which are derived from concepts about the nature of an individual's relationship to the state, and the state's obligation to safeguard the rights of the individual. See, for example, Thomas Paine, *The Rights of Man* (1791–2).

15. *West Indian ethics*: i.e. white West Indian. White West Indians were often looked down upon by Europeans. See Richard Cumberland's comedy *The West Indian* (1771) and Frances Burney's manuscript play *A Busy Day* (1801) for dramatic representations of white West Indians and English attitudes towards them. For a novelistic representation, see *Constantia Neville; or, The West Indian* by Helena Wells (1800).

16. *argumentum ad gubernatorem*: the argument to the governor.

17. *termagant*: a savage, violent or quarrelsome person.

18. *the lower animals*: perhaps a reference to eighteenth-century pseudo-scientific texts, in which 'Negros' were frequently compared to apes and other animals. This is the polygenist argument, i.e. that 'Negroes' and white people belong to separate species (as opposed to the monogenist argument in which all people belong to the same species). See Edward Long's *History of Jamaica*, II: 336, for an example of polygenist theory.

19. *licentious, and even depraved in her conduct*: Pringle has cut this allegation, probably for fear that it would offend the moral sensibilities of his Christian readers.

20. *an iniquitous colonial law*: Pringle is referring to the legal precedent set by the Mansfield Judgment of 1772, whereby a slave was free only while s/he remained in England. See Introduction, 'The Black Community and the Law'.

21. *the Cage*: see note 48, above.

22. *a connection with a white person, a Capt. —*: this is presumably Captain Abbot: see note 26, above.

23. *Stoke Newington, and Peckham, and Aldermanbury*: in north, south and east London respectively, presumably various headquarters of the Anti-Slavery Society.

24. *Mr M'Queen of Glasgow*: James McQueen was the editor of the *Glasgow Courier* and an opponent of emancipation. In 1831 he published an article in *Blackwood's Edinburgh Magazine* (no. 187, vol. 30, November 1831, pp. 744–64), 'The Colonial Empire of Great Britain', in which he claimed that Mary Prince was the tool of 'the prowling anti-colonial fry in London', including Thomas Pringle. McQueen refutes Prince's narrative and attacks Thomas

Pringle and Joseph Phillips ('this anti-colonial fungus'). In February 1833 Pringle successfully sued Thomas Cadell, the publisher of *Blackwood's*, for libel and was awarded £5 damages.

25. *report of the 'Ladies' Society of Birmingham for the relief of British Negro Slaves'*: the Birmingham Female Society for the Relief of British Negro Slaves, formerly the Ladies' Society, was one of many regional outlets of the Anti-Slavery Society whose mission was 'the melioration of the condition of the unhappy children of *Africa*, and especially of Female Negro Slaves, who, living under the British Dominions, receive from British hands their lot of bitterness' ('Third Report of the Female Society', 1828). The Birmingham Female Society was involved in fund-raising and consciousness-raising activities, and they maintained strong links with the main London branch of the Anti-Slavery Society. Clare Midgley writes that '[t]he Female Society of Birmingham was the first, the largest, the most influential and the longest lasting of the associations, and it played a key role in [the establishment of a network of ladies' societies]' (*Women Against Slavery. The British Campaigns, 1780–1870*, London: Routledge, 1992, pp. 44–5).

The minutes for the meeting held on 7 April 1829 include an extract of a letter from Thomas Pringle asking for funds, and the Female Society accordingly sent him the sum of £50 (acknowledged by him in July 1830: see 'Minute Book of the Ladies' Society for the Relief of Negro Slaves 1825–1852', Birmingham Public Library Archive, pp. 83, 103). The Birmingham Female Society also became involved in Mary Prince's cause: see Introduction, 'The *History* as Propaganda'.

The report from which Pringle is quoting here is no longer extant, but the 'Minute Book of the Ladies' Society for the Relief of Negro Slaves 1825–1832' includes the letter which is more detailed than the extract given here. Joseph Phillips was arrested and brought before the House of Assembly in Antigua for his involvement in Anti-Slavery activities. He was imprisoned for five months, but after his release he was re-arrested for debt 'which', according the letter included in the minutes, 'he was only prevented from paying by his loss of business and the ruinous proceedings against him'. The letter continues: '"It was by much entreaty" [Phillips writes] "that the marshal would allow me half an hour in custody of the Jailer, to go and see my dying mother-in-law and family after near five months absence! The tears of my wife and children was [*sic*] almost more than I could support, when I was again dragged to jail."' The Ladies' Society was evidently moved by this emotional account, and they unanimously voted that £15 should be sent 'for the relief of the individual' ('Minute Book 1825–1852', 95–6).

26. *Mary James*: Prince has taken her husband, Daniel James's name. In the petition presented to Parliament in June 1829, she is referred to as '*Molly Wood*', as well as '*Mary Princess* or *James*'. See Appendix Two.

27. *4, Keppel Street*: in Bloomsbury, central London.

28. *her chief faults . . . self-importance*: Clare Midgley notes that the 'faults' that Pringle lists here are precisely the qualities which enabled Prince to stand up to her owners and to campaign for her freedom. Midgley argues that because the Pringles wanted the rebellious slave to transform into an obedient servant, they underplayed her resistance by presenting her as a victim. 'Thus black agency in undermining slavery is devalued, and under the auspices of the Anti-Slavery Society, freedom is gained as the gift of white philanthropists who leave class relations undisturbed' (Midgley, 90).

29. *as black in character as in complexion*: the contrast between black body and white soul was frequently made in Abolitionist literature of this period. See, for example: William Blake, 'The Little Black Boy': 'My mother bore me in the southern wild / And I am black, but O! my soul is white / White as an angel is the English child, / But I am black, as if bereav'd of light' (*Blake: The Complete Poems*, New York: Longman, 1989, p. 58); William Cowper, 'The Negro's Complaint': 'Fleecy looks and black complexion / Cannot forfeit Nature's claim; / Skins may differ, but Affection / Dwells in White and Black the same' (*Poems*, III: 13).

30. *'absolute chattels'*: Pringle is correct to point out that slave owners regarded their slaves as property. In 1783, the case of *Gregson* v. *Gilbert* (known as the *Zong* case), drew widespread publicity to this aspect of slavery. During a voyage from West Africa to Jamaica, the Captain of the slave ship *Zong* decided to throw 131 slaves overboard because he did not think that there were sufficient supplies of food and water to last the journey. The shipowners subsequently tried to claim insurance for the 131 slaves (£30 each), since 'the Blacks were property' according to the law. The case came before Lord Justice Mansfield in 1783, but the outcome of the trial is not known. See James Walvin, *Black Ivory. A History of British Slavery* (London: Fontana Press, 1993), pp. 16–20.

31. *a residence . . . in a slave colony*: Pringle is referring to the six years he spent in South Africa.

32. *reports of the Fiscal of Berbice*: the *Anti-Slavery Monthly Reporter* (see 'Notes on the Footnotes', note g, below) of June 1825 lists details of the mistreatment of slaves in Berbice, Guyana. Atrocities reported include severe floggings and brutal punishments, white men raping their slaves, lack of food and overwork. The report concludes: 'The people of Great Britain cannot remain unaffected by such enormities perpetrated on their helpless fellow-subjects; nor can they continue to tolerate these fiscal regulations by which they are made to pay, in bounties and protecting duties, for the cost of this bloody and murderous system.'

33. *the Mauritius horrors*: the *Anti-Slavery Monthly Reporter* of January 1829 gives 'A Picture of Negro Slavery Existing in Mauritius', compiled by a member of the Society for the Conversion of Slaves.

34. *the case of Mr and Mrs Moss of the Bahamas*: a report in the *Anti-Slavery Monthly Reporter* of April 1829, 'Cruelties of Mr and Mrs Moss, of the Bahamas, towards a Female Slave'. The report describes the trial of the slave girl, Kate, who was accused of theft and disobedience. She was confined in the stocks for seventeen days and she had red pepper rubbed in her eyes, after which she developed a fever, was flogged by the overseer and died. Her owners, the Mosses of the Bahamas, were not accused of her murder, but sentenced to five months' imprisonment and a £300 fine. The *Anti-Slavery Monthly Reporter* protests against the intervention of the Governor of Bermuda on behalf of the Mosses.

35. *Eleanor Mead*: the case of Eleanor Mead, 'a mulatto female slave' living in Jamaica, was reported in the *Anti-Slavery Monthly Reporter* in August 1831. Her mistress ordered that she should be given fifty-eight lashes, humiliated and shackled. She managed to escape with her daughter and lodged a complaint with a local magistrate because thirty-nine lashes was the maximum legal punishment in Jamaica. However, she was sent back to her mistress and her complaint was not upheld because it was impossible to prove from her injuries how many lashes she had received.

36. *Henry Williams*: the *Anti-Slavery Monthly Reporter* of August 1830 reports that Henry Williams was sent to the workhouse where he was flogged until he was nearly dead for preferring the Methodist chapel to the Anglican church. The reporter is uncertain as to 'whether he had survived this atrocious act of barbarity'.

37. *the Rev. Mr Bridges and Kitty Hylton, in Jamaica*: the *Anti-Slavery Monthly Reporter* of September 1830 gives an account of 'the Slave Kitty Hylton's complaint against her Master, the Rev. G. W. Bridges', another case of ill-treatment in Jamaica. After a brutal, unprovoked beating, Kitty Hylton escaped from her master and lodged complaints with two magistrates, one of whom recognized the severity of the case and investigated it further. The Anti Slavery Society entered into a dispute with Bridges' defenders, and the case was reported in subsequent numbers of the *Reporter*. It was decided not to prosecute Bridges.

38. *the cane culture of Mauritius and Jamaica*: the growing of sugar cane in these places, rather than the ethos of the plantations.

39. *predial*: of farms or land (as opposed to cane culture).

40. *Dr Walsh . . . 'Notices of Brazil'*: Pringle is referring to the Rev. Robert Walsh's *Notices of Brazil in 1828 and 1829* (2 vols, London, 1830) which contains a section on the state of slavery in Brazil (II: 313–35). Robert Walsh (1772–1852) was an Irish curate and 'miscellaneous writer' (*DNB*) who travelled to Rio de Janeiro in 1828. His investigations into the extent of the slave trade in Brazil led to his appointment to a place on the Committee of the Society for the Abolition of the Slave Trade, which is presumably where he met Pringle.

41. *Pandora's box*: According to Hesiod, Pandora was the first woman created by Zeus, along with a box or a storage jar in which all evils and diseases were kept. Her husband Epimetheus opened the box, releasing all the evils into the world and leaving only hope at the bottom.

42. *bridewell*: a place of forced labour; gaol; prison.

43. *Russian knout*: scourge, often used in Russia.

44. *Governo*: in Brazil.

45. *Lord Stowell's decision in the case of the slave Grace*: see Introduction, 'The Black Community and the Law'.

46. *that qualified degree of freedom*: again referring to the Mansfield Judgment (1772), which set the precedent whereby a slave was free in England but not in the colonies. See Introduction, 'The Black Community and the Law'.

47. *a minor species of slave trading*: Pringle deploys a similar argument to that used by Grace Jones's advocates, namely that once a slave has been tacitly granted her freedom on coming to England, it is a form of slave trading (illegal since 1807) to re-enslave her by taking her back to the colonies.

48. *trepanning*: to *trepan*, in this sense, is to catch or beguile.

Notes on the Footnotes

a. *thrown into a loathsome jail*: in the *Anti-Slavery Monthly Reporter*, no. 74 (see note b, below), Joseph Phillips reports that he was imprisoned for 375 days in Antigua and was financially ruined as a consequence, because of his support for the Anti-Slavery movement.

b. *the Anti-Slavery Reporter, No. 74, p. 69*: in this issue it is reported that at a meeting in Bury St Edmunds in January 1831, Joseph Phillips, 'in a speech of considerable length, detailed the circumstances of his own persecution in Antigua, and gave his testimony against the evils of slavery'. Phillips reports that he was imprisoned for over a year because he advocated 'the cause of the unfortunate beings whose sufferings he had witnessed during a residence of twenty-seven years in the West Indies'. See note g, below, for the *Anti-Slavery Monthly Reporter*.

c. *After the preceding pages were printed*: this inserted footnote is altered in the third edition, but most of the variations are insignificant. However, in the third edition Pringle is more outspoken in his criticism of the Woods: he calls them 'on the whole, fair, perhaps favourable, specimens of colonial character' in the first edition, but he removes the adjective 'favourable' in the third.

d. *the Rev. J. Curtin*: in her narrative, Prince says that Curtin was the priest at the English church in Antigua who would not accept her into the congregation without written permission from Wood.

e. *catechumen*: a new convert under instruction before baptism; young Christian preparing for confirmation.

f. *If such things . . . what will be done in the dry?*: Ezekiel 17: 24: 'And all the trees of the field shall know that I the LORD have brought down the high tree, have exalted the low tree, have dried up the green tree and have made the dry tree to flourish.'

g. *Anti-Slavery Reporter*: the *Anti-Slavery Monthly Reporter* documented the abuse of slaves in the colonies, as well as reporting on local Anti-Slavery Society meetings, and surveying the opposition literature. The edition of April 1829 contains the following statement of intent:

> We shall . . . have before us a mass of suffering which may well make us shudder when we reflect that it has been inflicted, and is still proceeding, under British authority; and that therefore we, – this nation, – stand answerable for it all, before Him who claims the prerogative of being the avenger of the oppressed. Before Him and before the public do we again solemnly pledge ourselves, without fear of favour for any individuals, whether high or low, who participate in this CRIME to excell ourselves to the utmost, in vindicating the indefeasible claims of these unfinished and outcast children of humanity to the rights of British subjects; to equal laws; to justice; to freedom; and to all the blessings of the gospel.

APPENDIX (pp. 64–5)

1. *'Birmingham Ladies' Society for Relief of Negro Slaves'*: see 'Supplement', note 25, above. Margaret Pringle's letter was read aloud at the Society's sixth Annual Meeting in April 1831.

2. *Ashton Warner*: another slave who sought assistance from the Anti-Slavery Society. The Birmingham Female Society for the Relief of British Negro Slaves donated £5 to Ashton Warner and they allocated the same sum for Mary Prince at the same time. The minutes of the sixth Annual Meeting in April 1831 note the following resolution:

That five pounds be appropriated by this Society to originate a Fund for the support of Mary Prince, and that a similar sum be remitted towards the ransom of the enslaved Widow and Child of the recently deceased Negro, Ashton Warner, who on his death bed, recommended that the proceeds of a Narrative of his sufferings, which had been perused by a Friend to the cause, should be devoted to their enfranchisement (provided the amount be sufficiently considerable) and to the benefit of his aged Mother. This Society anxiously hope [*sic*] that the afflicting circumstances which have induced these appropriations will plead powerfully with other kindred institutions [Ladies' Associations] and that the example will be extensively imitated ['Minute Book 1825–1852', 109].

3. *Miss Martha Browne*: possibly the sister of Margaret Pringle (née Brown).

NARRATIVE OF LOUIS ASA-ASA

1. *a writ of Habeas Corpus*: writ requiring the body of the person to be brought before the judge or into court to ascertain the lawfulness of the restraint.

2. *Lord Wynford*: William Draper Best, first Baron Wynford (1767–1845). Knighted 1819, puisne judge, and called to the House of Lords in 1829, where he was one of the deputy speakers and a vehement supporter of the Tory party and opponent of the Reform Bill.

3. *Hampstead*: in north London.

4. *Sierra Leone*: a country in West Africa, bordered by Guinea and Liberia. First colonized by the British in 1787 as a settlement for Africans freed from slavery.

5. *a country called Bycla, near Egie*: I have been unable to locate these places.

6. *Adinyês*: again, I cannot find this name, which presumably refers to a local, rival tribe.

7. *carried away all the people whom they did not kill*: kidnapping was common practice in West Africa during the eighteenth century, and captives were often sold by locals to European slave traders. See, for example, Olaudah Equiano's account of his kidnapping with his sister (Equiano, 47). James Walvin calculates that upwards of 70 per cent of slaves had been kidnapped (Walvin, *Black Ivory*, 26).

8. *English guns*: Europeans traded guns for slaves in West Africa (see Walvin, *Black Ivory*, 27).

9. *till we got to England*: Asa-Asa's case is unusual: rather than being transported from West Africa to the Caribbean by French traders (the notorious Middle Passage) it seems that he was brought to England where he evidently escaped.

APPENDIX ONE

The following poems, dealing with the subject of slavery in South Africa, are taken from The Poetical Works of Thomas Pringle, with a Sketch of His Life *(London, 1838).*

THE BECHUANA BOY

I sat at noontide in my tent,
    And looked across the Desert dun,
Beneath the cloudless firmament
    Far gleaming in the sun,
When from the bosom of the waste
A swarthy Stripling came in haste,
With foot unshod and naked limb;
And a tame springbok followed him.

With open aspect, frank yet bland,
    And with a modest mien he stood,
Caressing with a gentle hand
    That beast of gentle brood;
Then, meekly gazing in my face,
Said in the language of his race,
With smiling look yet pensive tone,
'Stranger – I'm in the world alone!'

'Poor boy!' I said, 'thy native home
    Lies far beyond the Stormberg blue:
Why hast thou left it, boy! to roam
    This desolate Karroo?'

His face grew sadder while I spoke;
The smile forsook it; and he broke
Short silence with a sob-like sigh,
And told his hapless history.

'I have no home!' replied the boy:
    'The Bergenaars – by night they came.
And raised their wolfish howl of joy,
        While o'er our huts the flame
Resistless rushed; and aye their yell
Pealed louder as our warriors fell
In helpless heaps beneath their shot:
– One living man they left us not!

'The slaughter o'er, they gave the slain
    To feast the foul-beaked birds of prey;
And, with our herds, across the plain
        They hurried us away –
The widowed mothers and their brood.
Oft, in despair, for drink and food
We vainly cried: they heeded not,
But with sharp lash the captive smote.

'Three days we tracked that dreary wild,
    Where thirst and anguish pressed us sore;
And many a mother and her child
        Lay down to rise no more.
Behind us, on the desert brown,
We saw the vultures swooping down;
And heard, as the grim night was falling,
The wolf to his gorged comrade calling.

'At length was heard a river sounding
    'Midst that dry and dismal land,
And, like a troop of wild deer bounding,
        We hurried to its strand –
Among the maddened cattle rushing;
The crowd behind still forward pushing,
Till in the flood our limbs were drenched,
And the fierce rage of thirst was quenched.

'Hoarse-roaring, dark, the broad Gareep
  In turbid streams was sweeping fast,
Huge sea-cows in its eddies deep
    Loud snorting as we passed;
But that relentless robber clan
Right through those waters wild and wan
Drove on like sheep our wearied band:
– Some never reached the farther strand.

'All shivering from the foaming flood,
  We stood upon the stranger's ground,
When, with proud looks and gestures rude,
    The White Men gathered round:
And there, like cattle from the fold,
By Christians we were bought and sold,
'Midst laughter loud and looks of scorn –
And roughly from each other torn.

'My Mother's scream, so long and shrill,
  My little Sister's wailing cry,
(In dreams I often hear them still!)
    Rose wildly to the sky.
A tiger's heart came to me then,
And fiercely on those ruthless men
I sprang. – Alas! dashed on the sand,
Bleeding, they bound me foot and hand.

'Away – away on prancing steeds
  The stout man-stealers blithely go,
Through long low valleys fringed with reeds,
    O'er mountains capped with snow,
Each with his captive, far and fast;
Until yon rock-bound ridge we passed,
And distant stripes of cultured soil
Bespoke the land of tears and toil.

'And tears and toil have been my lot
  Since I the White Man's thrall became,
And sorer griefs I wish forgot –
    Harsh blows, and scorn, and shame!

Oh, Englishman! thou ne'er canst know
The injured bondman's bitter woe,
When round his breast, like scorpions, cling
Black thoughts that madden while they sting!

'Yet this hard fate I might have borne,
    And taught in time my soul to bend,
Had my sad yearning heart forlorn
        But found a single friend:
My race extinct or far removed,
The Boor's rough brood I could have loved;
But each to whom my bosom turned
Even like a hound the black boy spurned.

'While, friendless thus, my master's flocks
    I tended on the upland waste,
It chanced this fawn leapt from the rocks,
        By wolfish wild-dogs chased:
I rescued it, though wounded sore
And dabbled in its mother's gore;
And nursed it in a cavern wild,
Until it loved me like a child.

'Gently I nursed it; for I thought
    (Its hapless fate so like to mine)
By good Utíko it was brought
        To bid me not repine, –
Since in this world of wrong and ill
One creature lived that loved me still,
Although its dark and dazzling eye
Beamed not with human sympathy.

'Thus lived I, a lone orphan lad,
    My task the proud Boor's flocks to tend;
And this poor fawn was all I had
        To love, or call my friend;
When suddenly, with haughty look
And taunting words, that tyrant took
My playmate for his pampered boy,
Who envied me my only joy.

'High swelled my heart! – But when the star
　　Of midnight gleamed, I softly led
My bounding favourite forth, and far
　　　　Into the Desert fled.
And here, from human kind exiled,
Three moons on roots and berries wild
I've fared; and braved the beasts of prey,
To 'scape from spoilers worse than they.

'But yester morn a Bushman brought
　　The tidings that thy tents were near;
And now with hasty foot I've sought
　　　　Thy presence, void of fear;
Because they say, O English Chief,
Thou scornest not the Captive's grief:
Then let me serve thee, as thine own –
For I am in the world alone!'

Such was Marossi's touching tale.
　　Our breasts they were not made of stone:
His words, his winning looks prevail –
　　　　We took him for 'our own.'
And One, with woman's gentle art,
Unlocked the fountains of his heart;
And love gushed forth – till he became
Her Child in every thing but name.

THE CAPTIVE OF CAMALÚ

O Camalú – green Camalú!
　　'Twas there I fed my father's flock,
Beside the mount where cedars threw
　　At dawn their shadows from the rock;
There tended I my father's flock
　　Along the grassy-margined rills,
Or chased the bounding bontèbok
　　With hound and spear among the hills.

Green Camalú! methinks I view
    The lilies in thy meadows growing;
I see thy waters bright and blue
    Beneath the pale-leaved willows flowing;
I hear, along the valleys lowing,
    The heifers wending to the fold,
And jocund herd-boys loudly blowing
    The horn – to mimic hunters bold.

Methinks I see the umkóba-tree
    That shades the village-chieftain's cot;
The evening smoke curls lovingly
    Above that calm and pleasant spot.
My father? – Ha! – I had forgot –
    The old man rests in slumber deep:
My mother? – Ay! she answers not –
    Her heart is hushed in dreamless sleep.

My brothers too – green Camalú,
    Repose they by thy quiet tide?
Ay! there they sleep – where White Men slew
    And left them – lying side by side.
No pity had those men of pride,
    They fired the huts above the dying! –
– White bones bestrew that valley wide –
    I wish that mine were with them lying!

I envy you by Camalú,
    Ye wild harts on the woody hills;
Though tigers there their prey pursue,
    And vultures slake in blood their bills.
The heart may strive with Nature's ills,
    To Nature's common doom resigned:
Death the frail body only kills –
    But Thraldom brutifies the mind.

Oh, wretched fate! – heart-desolate,
    A captive in the spoiler's hand,
To serve the tyrant whom I hate –
    To crouch beneath his proud command –

Upon my flesh to bear his brand –
   His blows, his bitter scorn to bide! –
Would God, I in my native land
   Had with my slaughtered brothers died!

Ye mountains blue of Camalú,
   Where once I fed my father's flock,
Though desolation dwells with you,
   And Amakósa's heart is broke,
Yet, spite of chains these limbs that mock,
   My homeless heart to you doth fly, –
As flies the wild-dove to the rock,
   To hide its wounded breast – and die!

Yet, ere my spirit wings its flight
   Unto Death's silent shadowy clime,
Utíko! Lord of life and light,
   Who, high above the clouds of Time,
Calm sittest where yon hosts sublime
   Of stars wheel round thy bright abode,
Oh, let my cry unto Thee climb,
   Of every race the Father-God!

I ask not Judgments from thy hand –
   Destroying hail, or parching drought,
Or locust-swarms to waste the land,
   Or pestilence, by famine brought;
I say the prayer Jankanna taught,
   Who wept for Amakósa's wrongs –
'Thy kingdom come – thy Will be wrought –
   For unto Thee all Power belongs.'

Thy Kingdom come! Let Light and Grace
   Throughout all lands in triumph go;
Till pride and strife to love give place,
   And blood and tears forget to flow;
Till Europe mourn for Afric's woe,
   And o'er the Deep her arms extend
To lift her where she lieth low –
   And prove indeed her Christian Friend!

THE SLAVE DEALER

From ocean's wave a Wanderer came,
　　With visage tanned and dun:
His Mother, when he told his name,
　　Scarce knew her long-lost son;
So altered was his face and frame
　　By the ill course he had run.

There was hot fever in his blood,
　　And dark thoughts in his brain;
And oh! to turn his heart to good
　　That Mother strove in vain,
For fierce and fearful was his mood,
　　Racked by remorse and pain.

And if, at times, a gleam more mild
　　Would o'er his features stray,
When knelt the Widow near her Child,
　　And he tried with her to pray,
It lasted not – for visions wild
　　Still scared good thoughts away.

'There's blood upon my hands!' he said,
　　'Which water cannot wash;
It was not shed where warriors bled –
　　It dropped from the gory lash,
As I whirled it o'er and o'er my head,
　　And with each stroke left a gash.

'With every stroke I left a gash,
　　While Negro blood sprang high;
And now all ocean cannot wash
　　My soul from murder's dye;
Nor e'en thy prayer, dear Mother, quash
　　That Woman's wild death-cry!

'Her cry is ever in my ear,
    And it will not let me pray;
Her look I see – her voice I hear –
    As when in death she lay,
And said, "With me thou must appear
    On God's great Judgment-day!" '

'Now, Christ from frenzy keep my son!'
    The woeful Widow cried;
'Such murder foul thou ne'er hast done –
    Some fiend thy soul belied!' –
'– Nay, Mother! the Avenging One
    Was witness when she died!

'The writhing wretch with furious heel
    I crushed – no moral nigh;
But that same hour her dread appeal
    Was registered on high;
And now with God I have to deal,
    And dare not meet His eye!'

SLAVERY

On Slavery! thou art a bitter draught!
And twice accursèd is thy poisoned bowl,
Which taints with leprosy the White Man's soul,
Not less than his by whom its dregs are quaffed.
The Slave sinks down, o'ercome by cruel craft,
Like beast of burthen on the earth to roll.
The Master, though in luxury's lap he loll,
Feels the foul venom, like a rankling shaft,
Strike through his reins. As if a demon laughed.
He laughing, treads his victim in the dust –
The victim of his avarice, rage, or lust.
But the poor Captive's moan the whirlwinds waft
To Heaven – not unavenged: the Oppressor quakes
With secret dread, and shares the hell he makes!

TO OPPRESSION

Oppression! I have seen thee, face to face,
And met thy cruel eye and cloudy brow:
But thy soul-withering glance I fear not now;
For dread to prouder feelings doth give place
Of deep abhorrence. Scorning the disgrace
Of slavish knees that near thy footstool bow,
I also kneel – but with far other Vow
Do hail thee and thy herd of hirelings base.
I swear, while life-blood warms my throbbing veins,
Still to oppose and thwart with heart and hand
Thy brutalizing sway – till Afric's chains
Are burst, and Freedom rules the rescued land, –
Trampling Oppression and his iron rod.
– Such is the Vow I take – So help me God!

APPENDIX TWO

Printed below is the text of the Order of the Petition presented to Parliament on Mary Prince's behalf in June 1829, House of Commons Journals, *vol. 84, p. 404. In her edition of the* History *(London: Pandora, 1987, p. 116), Moira Ferguson errs in claiming that this text is itself the petition: in fact, it is only the report that the petition has been read in Parliament, and the petition itself appears to be no longer extant. It was possibly destroyed in a fire, or simply not considered worth preserving.*

A Petition of *Mary Princess* or *James*, commonly called *Molly Wood*, was presented and read, setting forth, That the Petitioner was born a Slave in the colony of *Bermuda*, and is now about forty years of age; That the Petitioner was sold some years ago for the sum of 300 dollars to Mr *John Wood*, by whom the Petitioner was carried to *Antigua*, where she has since, until lately resided as a domestic slave on his establishment; that in December 1826, the Petitioner, who is connected with the *Moravian* Congregation, was married in a *Moravian* Chapel at *Spring Gardens*, in the parish of *Saint John's*, by the *Moravian* minister, Mr *Ellensen*, to a free black, of the name of *Daniel James*, who is a carpenter at *Saint John's*, in *Antigua*, and also a member of the same congregation; that the Petitioner and the said *Daniel James* have lived together ever since as man and wife; that about ten months ago the Petitioner arrived in *London* with her master and mistress, in the capacity of nurse to their child; and that the Petitioner's master has offered to send her back in his brig to the *West Indies*, to work in the yard; that the Petitioner expressed her desire to return to the *West Indies*, but not as a slave, and has entreated her master to sell her, her freedom on account of her services as a nurse to his child, but he has refused, and still does refuse; further stating the particulars of her case; and praying the House to take the same into their consideration, and to grant such relief as to them may, under the circumstances, appear right.

Ordered, That the said Petition do lie upon the Table.

APPENDIX THREE

The following is an extract from Mary Prince's evidence given at the action of libel, Wood *v.* Pringle, *at the Court of King's Bench, Guildhall, 27 February 1833, and reported in* The Times, *Friday 1 March 1833.*

Mary Prince was the first witness called for the defence. She stated that she was now living in the Old Bailey, and was supported by the defendant. She had been a slave of the plaintiff, who purchased her for 300 dollars. When the plaintiff first purchased her she had to perform the general duties of a servant in the house, and was afterwards employed in washing. She afterwards became ill with St Anthony's fire and with the rheumatism. Her leg was much swoln and she could not walk without help. She slept at that time in one of the outhouses where there were swarms of bugs. A Mrs Green, who lived in the next yard, heard her cries in the outhouse; and she sent to her an old slave who used to bring her soup when she was ill. The doctor who attended her ordered her hot water. Brista, the cook, brought her dinner to the door of the outhouse, and then left her. The outhouse was very wet when it rained. The bed was stuffed with grass. The outhouse contained besides the bed a bench, which witness had brought from Bermuda, and a little old table. Witness seldom went out, and when she did go she walked with a stick a few yards from the outhouse. Letty occupied the adjoining room, and witness moved in there to the bath. Letty's room was better than her's. Dr McGoul saw her in that room. Mrs Wood never visited witness in either room. Witness had a pig given to her for some money which was owing to her by a woman. She complained of this mode of payment to Mrs Wood. Mr Wood was sent for, and he hit witness two knocks, and told the woman to take the witness before a magistrate. On going before the magistrate the woman stated that Mr Wood would not let her rest until she had made a complaint. Mr Wood's nephew, Mr Judkins, attended for Mr Wood before the magistrate, who dismissed the complaint, and witness was afterwards flogged with a cat-o'-nine-tails. She bled very much. The next morning she saw Mr Wood, and begged him to sell her. She was afterwards taken before another magistrate, who decided in her favour. Mr Wood and his family afterwards removed to a place called the Point. Witness had all the washing to do there. Mrs Wood frequently called her a spawn, and a good-for-nothing devil. On one occasion Mrs Wood followed her foot after foot, and scolded and rated. Mr Wood was sent for, and he gave her a note to go and look for a person to buy her. The following day Mr Wood beat her with a horsewhip. Martha Wilcox complained to Mrs Wood, and Mrs Wood said she would send for Mr Wood, to give her 50 lashes; that she had been used to the whip, and should have it then. Mr Wood then beat her all over her body. She was 'joined by the Moravians' to Daniel James, who lived a short distance from Mr Wood's house. Mr Wood did not know of her marriage for three or four months. Mr Burchell, a cooper, told him of it. Mr Wood licked her for it. He gave her about 50 lashes, swore at her, and said he would not have a nigger man's clothes washed in the same tub with his. Mr Burchell applied to purchase her, but Mr Wood would not sell her. She and her husband were always very loving, but her mistress was fretful about it, and said she did not do work enough. Witness came over to England with Mrs Wood, and had to take care of the child for her. On the passage Mrs Wood told her she did not mean to treat her any better when she got to England. Witness was very ill on the passage with the rheumatism. She had all the washing to do in Leigh-street. After some time an old woman was hired, but witness continued to wash. She on one occasion said she wished they had sold her in Antigua, and not brought her to England. The plaintiff was in a great passion and turned her out of doors. Mrs Wood never spoke to her kindly afterwards. She was always scolding her, calling her a devil, a black devil, and a spawn, and said she wanted to be a lady. Once, when she was so ill that she could not wash some clothes which had been given to her, the plaintiff told her that if she did not go away he would send her in the brig the next day to Antigua. She asked him to let her have her freedom, which he refused, saying she was free in England here, and as she liked to go out she might see what freedom would do for her in England. He told her that if she liked to return to Antigua she might and take the consequences. She stayed in the house for some time after the cook, a Mulatto woman, had gone away. When witness left the plaintiff's house the plaintiff gave her a paper which she gave to Mr Stephen, the defendant's attorney. The cook read to her the paper, of which the plaintiff took a copy. She (witness) once lived with a Captain Abbot. The witness was here questioned as to a statement made by the plaintiff in a letter from him to the governor's secretary, published in the pamphlet, charging her with gross immorality, and she denied the truth of the statement. The history of her life was written down by Miss Strickland at her (witness's) request; and she told that lady the truth.

Cross-examined. – The defendant was paying her 10s or 12s a week. He did this when she was out of place, and had done it since June last. The plaintiff gave witness the note soon after they came to England, and she continued in the plaintiff's service two months afterwards. She did not take the note to Mr Stephen for some time. When she left the Bermudas for the West Indies she was about 26 years of age. She went with the plaintiff, who bought her at her own request after about a year. Some years afterwards, when the plaintiff was about to sell her, she went on her knees and entreated Mrs Wood to persuade him not to sell her. She did not mention that fact to Miss Strickland. The plaintiff's eldest daughter did not teach her to read the Bible; she was too wild. The youngest daughter taught her to read. She was christened by the Rev. Mr Curtin, who told her to learn the Lord's Prayer. She got some of her neighbours to teach her it, and paid them. She knows Christmas time. The natives then have a 'stir up;' they dress in white, and dance; but if the ministers know of their dancing they prevent it. The plaintiff gave her a note to the Rev. Mr Curtin before she was christened, after she had begged for it and had been refused once. She was married about three years before she came to England. Her husband was a carpenter, a cooper, and a violin-player. The plaintiff gave him leave to live with her. She had lived seven years before with Captain Abbot. She did not live in the house with him, but slept with him sometimes in another hut which she had, in addition to her room in the plaintiff's yard. One night she found another woman in bed with the Captain in her house. This woman had pretended to be a friend of witness. (Laughter.) Witness licked her, and she was obliged to get out of bed. (A laugh.) The captain laughed, and the woman said she had done it to plague witness. Witness took her next day to the Moravian black leader, when she denied it, and witness then licked her again. (A laugh.) The woman then complained before a magistrate, Mr Justice Dyett; and when the story was told, they all laughed, and the woman was informed that she must never come there again with such tales, or she would be put into the stocks. Witness was also before the justice about beating a female slave, respecting a pig. Witness did not beat the woman, but she was punished as though she did, by the desire of Mr and Mrs Wood. She used to make a little money by selling small articles – such as coffee, yams, pigs, &c: and she used to take in washing. She came to England at her own request. She knew a free man of the name of Oyskman, who made a fool of her by telling her he would make her free. She lived with him for some time, but afterwards discharged him. That was when she first went to Antigua, and Oyskman was the first man who came to court her. She parted from Captain Abbot on his killing a man on board one of the plaintiff's vessels. She had been a member of the Moravian Society, and discharged herself in consequence of her connexion with Captain Abbot. She was kept out of the class for seven weeks. She told all this to Miss Strickland when that lady took down her narrative. These statements were not in the narrative published by the defendant. The slaves received presents at Christmas, and Mrs Wood gave witness clothes.

Re-examined. – She received no wages when in Leigh-street.

APPENDIX FOUR

Printed below is Thomas Pringle's article on the South African slave trade as it appeared in the Anti-Slavery Monthly Reporter *on 31 January 1827.*

SLAVERY AT THE CAPE OF GOOD HOPE

In the course of the last year an ordinance was promulgated in this colony, similar in its principle and provisions to that which has been established in Trinidad, for regulating the future treatment of slaves. It has generally been supposed in this country, that at the Cape of Good Hope the condition of the slaves was so mild as to call for no such interference on the part of Government. But it might have been assumed with certainty, that the accounts which led to such a conclusion were founded either in gross ignorance or in wilful misrepresentation. Slavery is an institution which, wherever it exists, must produce misery and degradation to all concerned in it; to the master as well as to the slave. Its effect in our West India colonies we are already familiar with. We shall hereafter be called to witness its still more horrid and revolting results as they are exhibited in the Mauritius. At present we confine ourselves to the Cape of Good Hope. Of the state of slavery in that colony, as it existed down to the month of January last, we are enabled to put our readers in possession of some authentic details which have been furnished by a colonist now in this country, on whose information we place implicit reliance. These details first appeared in the New Monthly Magazine for November last: we have satisfied ourselves of their truth, and we give them with confidence to our readers.

'*Cape of Good Hope, Jan. 5, 1826.*

'The mildness of Slavery at the Cape has been much dwelt upon by certain travellers, whose opinions on this subject, being re-echoed by the Quarterly Review and similar publications, seem to be generally admitted in England as perfectly just and incontrovertible. I am now satisfied, however, that the term, except in a very restricted sense, is altogether inapplicable. The general condition of slaves in this colony, compared with some others, (such, for example, as the Isle of France,) may, indeed, be correctly described as less deplorable: but with all its boasted alleviations, and in spite of every sweetening ingredient, slavery at the Cape is assuredly still a bitter and baleful draught.

'Should the comparative mildness of Cape slavery, however, be admitted, what a powerful argument does not this admission make for the speedy annihilation of human bondage throughout their colonies, by the powers of Christian Europe? If slaves are such wretched beings as I shall soon prove them to be, even at the Cape, what must be their condition in other colonies? What must be the condition of their masters?

'The slaves of this settlement can claim no respite from their masters' service, except on Sunday; and, as regards the household slaves, only partially on that day. They cannot legally marry, or legitimate their offspring, without the concurrence of their owner – a concurrence which his interests or his prejudices induce him, in almost every instance, to refuse. They cannot claim their freedom on presenting their purchase-money. They are frequently sold by public auction on the death or bankruptcy of their owners; and they are liable at all times, from casualty or from caprice, to be irretrievably separated from their wives, children, and dearest connections. At public sales the distressing spectacle of the wife torn from the husband, and the children from the parents, is so familiar as scarcely to interest the feelings of the spectators. Coarse jocularity and indecent merriment seldom fail, on such occasions, to be rudely bandied between the auctioneers and the rival bidders. Moreover, the slave is liable to be flogged whenever his owner's arrogant caprice may require it; and should he suffer ill-treatment from his master or the magistrate, he possesses in the laws (at least as they are usually administered) no security for obtaining redress.

'Yet the slave-holders in this colony continually exclaim – "Our slaves are as well fed and clothed as your English peasantry – infinitely better than your wretched Irish: in what respect, then, can they be considered objects of commiseration?" If such assertions were undeniable, the deduction drawn from them is not, on that account, the less fallacious. A few facts will show the futility of such arguments.

'In August, 1825, I was walking with a friend in the streets of Graaff-Reinett (a country town about five hundred miles from the capital), when we were accosted, in pretty good English, by a man of the Malay complexion. My companion, whom he addressed by name, asked how he came to know him. The man replied, that he had occasionally seen him at the house of his former master in Cape Town. On farther inquiry, he told us the following distressing story:—

'He was a slave, and had a wife and several children also in slavery. Being an expert waggon-driver, his master was offered a high price for him by a person from Graaff-Reinett. The offer was accepted, but the agreement concealed from the object of it. He was ordered to proceed with the waggon of his new purchaser into the interior, but given to understand that it was on his old master's business, and that he should return in a few months. On arriving at Graaff-Reinett, however, he was made acquainted with the transaction, and then found that he was for ever separated from all he cherished on earth. Even some little property in money and clothes, which he had hoarded and left behind him, he had never been able to recover, although two or three years had elapsed, and he had made repeated applications for it. The poor man appeared extremely dejected, and his melancholy tale was afterwards fully confirmed to me by other authority.

'Another recent illustration I shall extract from the letter of a friend (Mr J. F. Thomas, of the English India Company's Civil Service) who recently spent some years at the Cape.

' "While I was residing in the vicinity of Algon Bay, there came to the house, late at night, an old slave woman, who had fled from the ill usage of her mistress. She bore on her body marks of previous ill-treatment, having had three of her ribs broken at an earlier period of life, when she was in the possession of a former master. She was then in the family of an English resident, who had married a Dutch woman, and had been some years settled at —, within a few miles of Algon Bay. Her dress was a filthy untanned sheep-skin petticoat, with a few old rags about her head, and a dirty sheep-skin thrown over her shoulders. She had absconded from her master's house the preceding night; and after concealing herself in the day-time, had made her way, the night following, to the house where we resided.

' "The next morning, the son of the owner came to drive back the old woman before him. When I proposed to purchase from him the freedom of the slave, and stated her advanced age, he said that the work the old creature did was very considerable; and instanced her bringing daily to the house as much fire-wood on her back as any man could carry; adding, that, though he was willing to let the unhappy wretch have rest in her latter years, he could not part with her services under five hundred rix-dollars. Ultimately, however, he agreed to reduce her price to four hundred."

'The poor creature, thus emancipated, by the generosity of a stranger, now enjoys liberty and repose at the Missionary Institution of Bethelsdorp; but how seldom, among innumerable cases of equal hardship, can it happen that a solitary individual is thus relieved?

'Examples, such as these, of the wretchedness of slavery at the Cape, might be adduced without end, for they are of familiar and frequent occurrence. But since the authority of distinguished writers is so often brought forward to prove that in South Africa slavery is little more than a name, let us now produce the evidence of a celebrated traveller on the subject. Dr Sparrman, a man not less distinguished for his candour and integrity than for his eminence in science, and who, from the familiar footing on which his simple manners and mode of travelling placed him with every class of the inhabitants, was well qualified to form a correct judgment on this point, has given a very different picture of South African slavery from certain recent writers, who, in their slight and soothing descriptions of it, have either intentionally flattered the slave-holders, or their opportunities of observation had never extended beyond the well-dressed and pampered domestic slaves of Cape Town. Sparrman, on mentioning the murder of a planter in the interior by two of his slaves, makes the following just remarks:—

'"Yet whatever might be the real reason for committing this dreadful crime, I am convinced that it had its origin in the very essence and nature of the Slave Trade, in whatever manner and in whatever country it may be practised; a motive which I found had as much influence among the Christians, in many places, as among the Turks on the coast of Barbary, to induce the unhappy slaves, and still more their tyrannical masters, to behave very strangely; nay, sometimes, to be guilty of the most horrid cruelties. I have known some colonists, not only in the heat of their passion, but even deliberately and in cold blood, undertake themselves the low office (fit only for the executioner,) of not only flaying, for a trifling neglect, both the backs and limbs of their slaves by a peculiar slow lingering method, but likewise, outdoing the very tigers in cruelty, throw pepper and salt over the wounds. But what appeared to me more strange and horrid, was to hear a colonist, not only describe with great seeming satisfaction the whole process of this diabolical invention, but even pride himself on the practice of it; and rack his brains, in order to find sophisms in defence of it, as well as of the Slave Trade; in which occupation the important post he enjoyed in the colony, and his own interest, had engaged him. He was, however, a European by birth; of a free and civilized nation; and, indeed, gave evident proofs of possessing a kind and tender heart; so that, perhaps, it would be difficult to show any where a greater contradiction in the disposition of man, though in a world composed almost entirely of contradictions."

'Strange and horrid as this anomaly of character appeared to the worthy Sparrman, it is to this day as common as ever among slave-holders, – who, though in other respects humane and good-natured, become, by long practice, altogether callous and cruel-hearted in punishing their slaves. I have myself witnessed many striking instances of this. I have even known ladies, born and educated in England, charitable and benevolent in their general character, yet capable of standing over their female slaves while they were flogged, and afterwards ordering salt and pepper to be rubbed into their lacerated flesh! It is slavery, corrupting, hardening, brutalizing slavery, that produces this deplorable change in human feelings; and, while it degrades to the dust the wretched victim of oppression, vitiates, by a terrible re-action, the heart and character of the oppressor. – "Never be kind, nor speak kindly to a slave," said another English lady at the Cape, to a female relative of mine; "I have found," added she, "by experience in my own household, that nothing but hauteur and harshness will do with slaves."

'"There is a law, indeed (says Sparrman) existing in this colony, which prohibits masters from killing their slaves, or from flogging or otherwise chastising them with too great severity; but how is a slave to go to law with his master, who is, as it were, his sovereign; and who, by the same laws, has a right (or at least may, by dint of bribes, purchase that right) to have him flogged at the public whipping-post, not absolutely to death, indeed, yet not far from it; and this merely on the strength of the master's own testimony, and without any farther inquisition into the merits of the case? The master has, besides, so far his slave's life in his hands, that by rating and abusing him day by day, as likewise by proper 'domestic discipline,' as it is called, such as heavy iron chains, hard work, and little meat, he may without control, by little and little, though soon enough for his purpose, worry the poor fellow out of his life. In consequence of this, the unhappy slaves, who are frequently endued with finer feelings and nobler sentiments of humanity, though for the most part actuated by stronger passions than their masters, often give themselves up totally to despondency, and commit various acts of desperation and violence. Divers circumstances and considerations may, perhaps, concur to induce a wretch in this situation to exempt his tyrant from the dagger which he plunges in his own bosom; content with being thus able to put an end to his own misery, and at the same time to disappoint his greedy master of the profits arising from the sweat of his brow. A female slave, who had been just bought at a high price, and rather prematurely treated with severity by her mistress, who lived in the Roode-zand district, hanged herself the same night out of revenge and despair, just at the entrance of her new mistress's bedchamber. A young man and woman who were slaves at the Cape, and were passionately fond of each other, solicited their master, in conformity with the established custom, for his consent to their being united in wedlock, though all in vain, as from some whim or caprice he was induced absolutely to forbid it. The consequence was, that the lover was seized with a singular fit of despair; and having first plunged a dagger into the heart of the object of his dearest wishes, immediately afterwards put an end to his own life. But how many hundred instances, not less dreadful than these, might be produced to this purpose."*

* 'Sparrman's Voyage to the Cape of Good Hope,' vol. ii, p. 341.

'How indeed can it be wondered at, that hatred and revenge on the part of the slave, and suspicion and dislike on the part of the master, should be so generally the result of this unnatural relationship. And amidst the continual effervescence of such feelings, is it surprising that instances of masters flogging their slaves to death, of shooting them in a passion, or cases of still more cool-blooded and revolting atrocity, should occasionally occur? Or is it surprising, on the other hand, that desperate risings of the slaves to murder their masters, and their far more frequent attempts to destroy them secretly by poison, should be equally familiar at the Cape as in other slave colonies?

'That such occurrences are sufficiently frequent and familiar at the Cape, no one who has lived a few years in the colony will deny. It will be sufficient to refer merely to a few recent examples. In 1822, Mr Gebhardt, the son of a country clergyman, was executed for flogging to death one of his father's slaves. At that time there were five cases of slave murder before the deputy fiscal, all of a more aggravated character than that of this unfortunate young man, though he alone was punished capitally. A far more atrocious case occurred a few years previously (though from some cause or other not brought to capital conviction) of a monster, who actually roasted one of his slaves alive in an oven. In 1824, a young gentleman of my own acquaintance (an Englishman) shot one of his slaves in a passion, and was for this crime condemned by the court of circuit to one year's imprisonment.

'In October, 1824, two attempts of slaves to poison their mistresses occurred within my own circle of acquaintance. In the same year occurred the desperate outrage of a few slaves and Hottentots in the Bokkeveld, who being cruelly treated by their masters, and summarily flogged by the local magistracy, whenever they went to claim redress, at length rose with arms in their hands, and destroyed two or three of the colonists; for which crime several of them were hanged, and others condemned to work in irons for life. In the same year, or in the close of 1823, a slave woman, in the district of Graaff-Reinett, was convicted of having murdered her own child, in order to revenge herself upon her mistress, by whom she had been harshly used. I am not aware whether or not this unhappy wretch was executed, but I read the evidence on her trial at the time in the hands of the Deputy Fiscal.

'The following case occurred in 1822. The daughter of a respectable burgher, residing in Graaff-Reinett, was suspected of having murdered her illegitimate child, in order to conceal her disgrace. The Landdrost, Captain Stockenstrom, (an active and impartial magistrate,) after due investigation of the facts, apprehended the girl, together with one of the female slaves of the colony, and an old Hottentot woman who assisted at the accouchement. The prisoners were finally transmitted to Cape Town to be prosecuted by the Fiscal before the Court of Justice. It appeared from the evidence elicited on the trial, that the mother had either strangled the infant herself, or forced the slave by threats to do so; and that the slave had afterwards carried away and concealed the body. The court condemned the mother of the infant and the slave to capital punishment for the murder, and the Hottentot woman to twelve months imprisonment.

'From this sentence, the friends of the white woman appealed; and the governor, as judge of the Court of Appeals, reversed the sentence in her favour. She was consequently liberated; re-appeared among her acquaintance, as if nothing had occurred, and in a few months was married.

'But what became of the unhappy slave woman, who had been the accomplice of her young mistress in the crime? Who appealed in her behalf? Who implored mercy for her? Not her master: he endeavoured to impute to her all the guilt, and willingly surrendered her life as a ransom for that of his daughter. Not the members of the Court of Justice: they had, as they deemed, duly performed their functions, and would not interfere beyond them. Not the Court of Appeals: it had saved the free woman; it cared not for the slave. Not the public: there is no public voice heard at the Cape.

'The poor slave remained in jail; and was about to be sacrificed alone for a crime, in which (if she assisted at all) it was evident she was not the principal, but merely the blind accomplice of her mistress, whether from obsequious attachment or from servile fear. At this crisis, a friend of humanity – a casual visitor from India, heard of her pitiful case with interest and indignation. He visited her in prison, drew up a strong statement on the subject, and laid it before the governor. The governor, though he had previously passed it over unnoticed, was now moved; and the poor creature was saved.

'I have stated that mothers and children are often separated by being sold to different purchasers at the public sales. Examples of this are of daily occurrence; but one or two will sufficiently illustrate this part of the subject.

'Advertisement extracted from the Cape Gazette of Oct. 12, 1822:–

'"To be sold by auction, to the highest bidder, on the 14th instant, by order of the board of Orphan Masters, in such condition as will then be specified, the buildings on the Loan Place, Brood Kraal, at Berg River, district of Stellenbosch.

'"There will also be sold a female slave, named Candasa, of Mozambique, fifty-four years old, with her five children; Saphira, aged thirteen years; Eva, ten; Candasa, nine; Jannetje, seven; and Carlo, five; each to be put up separately."

'The following account of a scene of this kind, is extracted from the letter of a friend of the writer, while travelling in the interior of the Colony:–

' "Having learned that there was to be a sale of cattle, farm stock, &c. by auction, at a Veld-Cornet's in the vicinity, we halted our waggon one day for the purpose of procuring a fresh Spann of oxen. Among the stock of the farm sold, was a female slave and her three children. The two eldest children were girls, the one about thirteen years of age, and the other about eleven; the youngest was a boy. The whole family were exhibited together, but they were sold separately, and to different purchasers. The farmers examined them as if they had been so many head of cattle. While the sale was going on, the mother and her children were exhibited on a table, that they might be seen by the company, which was very large. There could not have been a finer subject for an able painter than this unhappy group. The tears, the anxiety, the anguish of the mother, while she met the gaze of the multitude, eyed the different countenances of the bidders, or cast a heart-rending look upon the children; and the simplicity and touching sorrow of the poor young ones, while they clung to their distracted parent, wiping their eyes, and half concealing their faces, – contrasted with the marked insensibility and jocular countenances of the spectators and purchasers, – furnished a striking commentary on the miseries of slavery, and its debasing effects upon the hearts of its abettors. While the woman was in this distressed situation she was asked 'Can you feed sheep?' Her reply was so indistinct that it escaped me; but it was probably in the negative, for her purchaser rejoined in a loud and harsh voice, 'Then I will teach you with the sjamboc.'* The mother and her three children were sold to three separate purchasers; and they were literally torn from each other. How just the remark of Cowper, –

'There is no flesh in man's obdurate heart –
It does not feel for man!' "

'The following notices of cases between masters and slaves, are extracted from the Annual Lists of trials before the Courts of Justice, and its Commissioners, inserted in the Cape Gazette; and are only a small selection out of a multitude of such cases, in Cape Town and its vicinity, between the years 1817 and 1822. Brief as these notices are, they may suffice, without any comment, to exhibit, in a distinct light, the degraded condition of men in slavery, (even in its mildest state,) and the striking inequality of the Colonial laws and Courts of Justice, as they practically affect them and their masters:–

Masters v. *Slaves.*	*Slaves* v. *Masters.*
'Jacob of Mozambique, slave of W. Servyntyn, for threatening the life of his master, and making resistance against the Veld-Cornet: condemned to be exposed	'Johannes J. Synders, for the cruel treatment of a slave, who was said to have died in consequence; condemned to six months imprisonment.

* A whip made of the Rhinoceros' hide.

to public view, made fast by a rope under the gallows; thereupon to be flogged, branded, and confined on Robben Island (to work in irons) for life.

'David, of Mozambique, slave of A. Laubscher, for an armed and violent attack upon his master: condemned to be hanged; which sentence received the sanction of the governor: Remitted, and returned to said master, with information to prisoner, on his release, that it is to his master's kind interference he owes his life, as the law certainly demanded the forfeit of it.

['N.B. Had the slave been hanged, it would have been a loss to his master of about 200l.]

'Louis, slave of D. Hugo, for wilfully wounding his master: condemned to be hanged. Sentence remitted by the acting governor.

'April, Slave of A. de Villiers, on a charge of murder: condemned to be hanged at the village of Stellenbosch, and his head and right hand to be cut off, and exposed to public view on a pole.

'Hendrik, slave of P. S. Tesselaar, on a charge of grossly ill-treating his wife, in consequence of which she was delivered of a dead child: condemned to be exposed to public view, with a rope round his neck, under the gallows: then scourged and branded; and afterwards to labour in irons, without wages, on the public works at Robben Island for life.

'Jasmyn, slave of Dirk Cloctè, on a charge of preferring a false complaint against the Landdrost of Stellenbosch, to His Majesty's Fiscal; condemned to be severely flogged.

'C. Jansen, European servant of J. R. Louw, on a charge of ill-treatment preferred against him by Diedrik and Joseph, slaves of said Low: condemned in a penalty of fifty rixdollars (3l. 15s.) on behalf of the poor's box at the Paarl.

'C. A. Marais, on a charge of ill-treatment, preferred against him by his female slave Kaatje: defendant sentenced in a penalty of twenty-five rix-dollars, and severely reprimanded.

'A. P. Zeeman and his wife, on a charge of serious ill-treatment, preferred against them by their female slave Theresa: by sentence said slave to be judicially sold, and never to come again into possession of defendants or their relatives.

'O. C. Mostert, for cruel treatment of a female slave, in consequence of which she died: condemned to be banished from this colony and its dependencies for twenty-five years.

'P. J. de Villiers, on a charge of ill-treatment of his slave April: condemned to a confinement of three months in the prison of Stellenbosch. Which sentence, however, his Excellency the Governor commuted to a pecuniary fine.

'P. S. Bosman, on a charge of ill-treatment, preferred against him by his slave July. The complaint having been proved groundless, the plaintiff condemned to be flogged. [This case exhibits the most usual result of complaints by slaves against their masters.]

'D. Malang, on a charge of excessive ill-treatment of one of his slaves, of which his death was the consequence. Defendant acquitted of said charge, and the plaintiff, Adam, condemned to be flogged.

'Asia, slave of Isaac Coetzee, for having brought forward a false charge against his mistress for ill-treatment of the female slave Diana, which was alleged to be the cause of her death: condemned to be severely flogged. .

'Saptoe, (a convict slave,) on a charge of secretly entering a house, with the presumed intention of stealing; prisoner condemned to be flogged, branded, and confined to labour ten years in irons.

'Johannes Tobias Laubscher, on a charge of ill-treatment preferred against him by his slaves Stephen, Marthinus, and Solon: the first and second plaintiffs sentenced to receive each thirty lashes, and the confinement suffered by the third deemed an adequate punishment. The defendant was also sentenced, for reasons moving the Court, in the penalty of thirty rix-dollars. (1l. 10s.)

'Such are a few – a very few specimens of the outrages continually recurring on the part either of the oppressor or the oppressed, in a country where slavery is said to assume its mildest aspect. Yet, wretched as is this state of reciprocal enmity and suspicion, still more deplorable, if possible, is the dreadfully demoralizing influence of slavery upon the young, alike of the free and the enthralled population. Marriage and baptism, systematically discouraged by the masters in general, are rare among the slaves. Promiscuous intercourse is common. Illicit connections with the white men are encouraged among the young female slaves – frequently even prescribed by their "Christian" owners. In Cape Town it is notorious as noon-day, that the rearing and educating of handsome female slaves, as objects of licentious traffic with the European, and especially with the rich Indian residents, is extensively practised among slave-holders. If such transactions are now managed with some greater regard to outward decorum than formerly, they are not on that account the less frequent; and I feel no hesitation in asserting, in the face of the authoritative dicta of the "Quarterly Review," that the practice of this disgraceful traffic is still common in the colony.*

'While the female slaves are thus bred up to prostitution, the reaction of their depravity upon the morals of the white population is equally obvious and frightful. Brought up from infancy in collision with a brutalized race of beings, from whom all enjoyments but those of the senses are debarred, what can the youth of either sex learn earliest but the knowledge of evil – the

---

* 'A writer in that Journal, in reviewing a little volume, entitled 'Notes on the Cape of Good Hope,' in 1821, endeavours to discredit the author's report of the state of morals, and the anecdotes he has given to illustrate the influence of slavery in destroying female delicacy. I *know*, however, that that author was correct both in his opinions and facts on this point; though I differ from him entirely in his estimate of the comparative happiness of the slave population.'

language and the lessons of licentiousness? Who that has resided at the Cape can be ignorant of the general and premature profligacy of manners among the young men? Who, indeed, but must be sensible that the ruling classes in every slave colony, are (and must necessarily be) depraved to an appalling extent by the early and uncontrolled indulgence of almost all the worst propensities of our nature? – by sensuality, unfeeling selfishness,* arrogance, rage, revenge? If the African colonists, as a body, are, notwithstanding all this, less corrupted than the mass of slave-holders in some other countries, they owe it chiefly to the comparatively limited extent of their slave population, and to the early marriages, and simpler and purer manners, of the majority of the country inhabitants. I wish not to speak of them harshly. There are, I am well convinced, a great number of pious, humane, and truly worthy people at the Cape, to whom the above observations do not in any respect apply. I am also convinced, that in spite of all their defects and disadvantages, the Cape Dutch, regarded as a body of men, possess many estimable qualities. If they have acquired many of an opposite description, it is because they have

---

* 'The influence of slavery, in hardening the feelings, and in destroying even the most powerful of our natural affections, is almost incredible. Such facts as masters selling their own children by slave women, are at the Cape far from unfrequent. I shall mention only one which occurred a few months ago. The wife of an extensive farmer (a person mentioned by Latrobe, and who resides about one hundred miles from Cape Town,) died in 1825, when, in conformity with the Dutch law of succession, the conjunct property was brought to a public sale, in order that the children might receive their respective shares. The old woman had exacted a promise from her husband on her death-bed, that he would emancipate certain slave-children in the household, and not allow them to be sold, because they were known to be the children of one of their own sons, who was now settled on a neighbouring estate. The old man, desirous to keep his promise, was resolutely opposed (incredible as it may seem) by his son, the very father of the children in question. The motive for this opposition to the dictates of nature – to his mother's dying request – and his father's solemn promise – was sordid avarice. If the children were not sold, he would lose his share of their price – of the price of his own flesh and blood! He insisted that they should be produced at the public sale. The law was on his side, and the father could not refuse his demand. But the old man's regard to his last promise to his deceased wife, and his indignation at his son's inhuman conduct, induced him to stand up at the sale, and after mentioning the above details to the whole assembly, to declare his determination to re-purchase the children himself at whatever price, and to grant them their freedom, as he had pledged himself to do. The old man's conduct was approved of, and no one offered to compete with him in bidding for the children; yet the relator of this anecdote, who was present on the occasion, heard neither surprise nor indignation expressed at the conduct of the son, nor any censure passed upon him, with the exception of a remark made by a Moravian missionary.'

been so long doubly debased by the curse of slavery, and the deprivation of a good constitution of government. Let England remove that unspeakable curse, and govern them as she should do, – and *then* I will venture to say with confidence of my fellow Colonists, that there is no moral or intellectual excellence, of which they will not speedily be found capable.'